BY CHARLES BUKOWSKI
AVAILABLE FROM ECCO

CHARLES BUKOWSKI

THE LAST NIGHT OF THE EARTH POEMS

ecco

An Imprint of HarperCollinsPublishers

Previously published by Black Sparrow Press

HarperCollins books may be purchased for educational, business, or sales promotional use. For information, please e-mail the Special Markets Department at SPsales@harpercollins.com.

First Ecco edition published in 2002.

ACKNOWLEDGMENTS

The author would like to thank the editors of the periodicals where some of these poems first appeared.

THE Library of Congress has catalogued a previous editions as follows:

Bukowski, Charles.
 The last night of the earth poems / Charles Bukowski.
  p. cm.
  ISBN 0-87685-864-7 :
  –ISBN 0-87685-863-9 (pbk.) :
  I. Title.
PS3552.U4L37   1992
814'.54—dc20   91-45022
                                                                    CIP

23 24 25 26 27 LBC 44 43 42 41 40

table of contents

1.

2.

4.

the last night of the earth poems

1

my wrists are rivers
my fingers are words

jam

that Harbor Freeway south through the downtown
area—I mean, it can simply become
unbelievable.

last Friday evening I was sitting there
motionless behind a wall of red taillights,
there wasn't even first gear movement
as masses of exhaust fumes
greyed the evening air, engines over-
heated
and there was the smell of a clutch
burning out
somewhere—
it seemed to come from ahead of me—
from that long slow rise of freeway where
the cars were working
from first gear to neutral
again and again
and from neutral back to
first gear.

on the radio I heard the news
of that day
at least 6 times, I was
well versed in world
affairs.
the remainder of the stations played a
thin, sick music.
the classical stations refused to come in
clearly
and when they did
it was a stale repetition of standard and
tiresome works.

I turned the radio off.
a strange whirling began in my
head—it circled behind the forehead, clock-

wise, went past the ears and around to the
back of the head, then back to the forehead
and around
again.
I began to wonder, is this what happens
when one goes
mad?

I considered getting out of my car.
I was in the so-called fast
lane.
I could see myself out there
out of my car
leaning against the freeway divider,
arms folded.
then I would slide down to a sitting
position, putting my head between
my legs.

I stayed in the car, bit my tongue, turned
the radio back on, *willed* the whirling to
stop
as I wondered if any of the others had to
battled against their
compulsions
as I did?

then the car ahead of me
MOVED
a foot, 2 feet, 3 feet!

I shifted to first gear . . .
there was MOVEMENT!
then I was back in neutral
BUT
we *had moved* from 7 to
ten feet.

hearing the world news for the
7th time,

it was still all bad
but all of us listening,
we could handle that too
because we knew
that there was nothing worse than
looking at
that same license plate
that same dumb head sticking up
from behind the headrest
in the car ahead of you
as time dissolved
as the temperature gauge leaned
more to the right
as the gas gauge leaned
more to the left
as we wondered
whose clutch was burning
out?

we were like some last, vast
final dinosaur
crawling feebly home somewhere,
somehow, maybe
to
die.

two toughs

at L.A. City College there were two toughs, me and Jed
Anderson.
Anderson was one of the best running backs in the
history of the school, a real breakaway threat
anytime he got the football.
I was pretty tough physically but looked at sports
as a game for freaks.
I thought a bigger game was challenging those
who attempted to teach
us.

anyhow, Jed and I were the two biggest lights on
campus, he piled up his 60, 70 and 80 yard
runs in the night games
and during the days
slouched in my seat
I made up what I didn't know
and what I did know
was so bad
many a teacher was made to
dance to it.

and one grand day
Jed and I
finally met.
it was at a little jukebox place
across from campus and
he was sitting with his
pals
and I was sitting with
mine.

"go on! go on! talk to him!"
my pals
urged.
I said, "fuck that gym
boy. I am one with

Nietzsche, let him come
over here!"

finally Jed got up to get a
pack of smokes from the
machine and one of my
friends asked,
"are you afraid of that
man?"

I got up and walked behind
Jed as he was reaching into the
machine
for his pack.

"hello, Jed," I
said.

he turned: "hello,
Hank."

then he reached into his
rear pocket,
pulled out a pint of
whiskey, handed it to
me.

I took a mighty hit,
handed it
back.

"Jed, what are you
going to do
after
L.A.C.C.?"

"I'm going to play
for Notre Dame."

then he walked back
to his table
and I walked back
to mine.

"what'd he say? what'd
he say?"

"nothing much."

anyhow, Jed never made it
to Notre Dame
and I never made it
anywhere
either—
the years just swept us
away
but there were others
who went
on, including one fellow
who became a famous
sports columnist
and I had to look at his
photo
for decades
in the newspaper
as I inherited those
cheap rooms
and those roaches
and those airless
dreary
nights.

but
I was still proud of that moment
back then
when Jed handed me
that pint
and
I drained

a third of it
with all the disciples
watching.
damn, there was no way
it seemed
we could ever
lose
but we did.

and it took me
3 or 4 decades to
move on just a
little.
and Jed,
if you are still here
tonight,
(I forgot to tell you
then)
here's a thanks
for that drink.

my German buddy

tonight
drinking Singha
malt liquor from
Thailand
and listening to
Wagner

I can't believe that
he is not in
the other
room
or around the
corner
or alive
someplace
tonight

and he is
of course
as I am taken
by the sound of
him

and little goosebumps
run along
both of my
arms

then a
chill

he's here

now.

happy birthday

when Wagner was an
old man
a birthday party was given
in his
honor
and a couple of
youthful
incidental compositions
were played.

afterwards
he asked,
"who wrote those?"

"you did," he was
told.

"ah," he responded,
"it's as I have always
suspected: death
then
does have some
virtue."

the telephone

will bring you people
with its ring,
people who do not know what to do with
their time
and they will ache to
infect you with
this
from a distance
(although they would prefer
to actually be in the same room
to better project their nullity upon
you).

the telephone is needed for
emergency purposes only.

these people are not
emergencies, they are
calamities.

I have never welcomed the ring of a
telephone.

"hello," I will answer
guardedly.

"this is Dwight."

already you can feel their imbecile
yearning to invade.
they are the people-fleas that
crawl the
psyche.

"yes, what is it?"

"well, I'm in town tonight and
I thought . . ."

"listen, Dwight, I'm tied up, I
can't . . ."

"well, maybe another
time?"

"maybe not . . ."

each person is only given so many
evenings
and each wasted evening is
a gross violation against the
natural course of
your only
life;
besides, it leaves an aftertaste
which often lasts two or three days
depending upon the
visitor.

the telephone is only for
emergency purposes.

it has taken me
decades
but I have finally found out
how to say
"no."

now
don't be concerned for them,
please:
they will simply dial another
number.

it could be
yours.

"hello," you will
say.

and they will say,
"this is Dwight."

and then
you
be
the kind
understanding
soul.

begging

like most of you, I've had so many jobs that
I feel as if I were gutted and my insides
thrown to the winds.
I've met some good people along the
way and also the
other kind.
yet when I think of all those
I have worked with—
even though decades have passed—
Karl
comes to mind
first.

I remember Karl: our jobs required we
both wear aprons
tied from behind and around
the neck with string.

I was Karl's underling.
"we got an easy job," he
told me.

each day as one by one our superiors arrived
Karl would make a slight bend at the waist,
smile, and with a nod of the head
greet each: "good morning Dr. Stein,"
or, "good morning Mr. Day" or
Mrs. Knight or if the lady was unattached
"good morning, Lilly" or Betty or Fran.

I never
spoke.

Karl seemed concerned at this and
one day he took me aside: "hey,
where the fuck else you going to get a

two hour lunch like we
do?"

"nowhere, I guess . . ."

"well, o.k., look, for guys like you and me,
this is as good as it can get, this is all
there is."

I waited.

"so look, it's hard to suck up to them at first, it
didn't come easy for me
but after a while I realized that it
didn't matter.
I just grew a shell.
now I've got my shell, got
it?"

I looked at him and sure enough he did look like he had
a shell, there was a mask-like look to his
face and the eyes were null, void and
undisturbed; I was looking at a weathered and
beaten conch.

some weeks went by.
nothing changed: Karl bowed and scraped and smiled
undaunted, perfect in his
role.
that we were *perishable*, perhaps didn't occur to
him
or
that greater gods might be
watching.

I did my
work.

then, one day, Karl took me
aside again.

"listen, Dr. Morely spoke to me
about you."

"yes?"

"he asked me what was wrong with
you."

"what did you tell
him?"

"I told him that you were
young."

"thanks."

upon receiving my next check, I
quit

but

still
had to
eventually settle for another similar
job
and
viewing the
new Karls
I finally forgave them all
but not myself:

being perishable sometimes makes a
man
strange
almost
unemployable

most
obnoxious—
no servant of
free
enterprise.

the feel of it

A. Huxley died at 69,
much too early for such a
fierce talent,
and I read all his
works
but actually
Point Counter Point
did help a bit
in carrying me through
the factories and the
drunk tanks and the
unsavory
ladies.
that
book
along with Hamsun's
Hunger
they helped a
bit.
great books are
the ones we
need.

I was astonished at
myself for liking the
Huxley book
but it did come from
such a rabid
beautiful
pessimistic
intellectualism,
and when I first
read *P.C.P.*
I was living in a
hotel room
with a wild and

crazy
alcoholic woman
who once threw
Pound's *Cantos*
at me
and missed,
as they did
with me.

I was working
as a packer
in a light fixture
plant
and once
during a drinking
bout
I told the lady,
"here, read this!"
(referring to
*Point Counter
Point.*)

"ah, jam it up
your ass!" she
screamed at
me.

anyhow, 69 seemed
too early for Aldous
Huxley to
die.
but I guess it's
just as fair
as the death of a
scrubwoman
at the same
age.

it's just that
with those who

help us
get on through,
then
all that light
dying, it works the
gut a bit—
scrubwomen, cab drivers,
cops, nurses, bank
robbers, priests,
fishermen, fry cooks,
jockeys and the
like
be
damned.

the greatest actor of our day

he's getting fatter and fatter,
almost bald
he has a wisp of hair
in the back
which he twists
and holds
with a rubber band.

he's got a place in the hills
and he's got a place in the
islands
and few people ever see
him.
some consider him the greatest
actor of our
day.

he has few friends, a
very few.
with them, his favorite
pastime is
eating.

at rare times he is reached
by telephone
usually
with an offer to act
in an exceptional (he's
told)
motion picture.

he answers in a very soft
voice:

"oh, no, I don't want to
make any more movies . . ."

"can we send you the
screenplay?"

"all right . . ."

then
he's not heard from
again.

usually
what he and his few friends
do
after eating
(if the night is cold)
is to have a few drinks
and watch the screenplays
burn
in the fireplace.

or
after eating (on
warm evenings)
after a few
drinks
the screenplays
are taken
frozen
out of cold
storage.
he hands some
to his friends
keeps some
then
together
from the veranda
they toss them
like flying saucers
far out
into the spacious

canyon
below.

then
they all go
back in
knowing
instinctively
that the screenplays
were
bad. (at least,
he senses it and
they
accept
that.)

it's a real good
world
up there:
well-earned, self-
sufficient
and
hardly
dependent
upon the
variables.

there's
all that time
to eat
drink
and
wait on death
like
everybody
else.

days like razors, nights full of rats

as a very young man I divided an equal amount of time between
the bars and the libraries; how I managed to provide for
my other ordinary needs is the puzzle; well, I simply didn't
bother too much with that—
if I had a book or a drink then I didn't think too much of
other things—fools create their own
paradise.

in the bars, I thought I was a tough, I broke things, fought
other men, etc.

in the libraries it was another matter: I was quiet, went
from room to room, didn't so much read entire books
as parts of them: medicine, geology, literature and
philosophy. psychology, math, history, other things, put me
off. with music I was more interested in the music and in the
lives of the composers than in the technical aspects . . .

however, it was with the philosophers that I felt a brotherhood:
Schopenhauer and Nietzsche, even old hard-to-read Kant;
I found Santayana, who was very popular at the time, to be
limp and a bore; Hegel you really had to dig for, especially
with a hangover; there are many I read who I have forgotten,
perhaps properly so, but I remember one fellow who wrote an
entire book in which he proved *that the moon was not there*
and he did it so well that afterwards you thought, he's
absolutely right, the moon is *not* there.

how the hell is a young man going to deign to work an
8 hour day when the moon isn't even there?
what else
might be missing?

and
I didn't like literature so much as I did the literary
critics; they were real pricks, those guys; they used
fine language, beautiful in its way, to call other

critics, other writers, assholes. they
perked me up.

but it was the philosophers who satisfied
that need
that lurked somewhere within my confused skull: wading
through their excesses and their
clotted vocabulary
they still often
stunned
leaped out
with a flaming gambling statement that appeared to be
absolute truth or damned near
absolute truth,
and this certainty was what I was searching for in a daily
life that seemed more like a piece of
cardboard.

what great fellows those old dogs were, they got me past
days like razors and nights full of rats; and women
bargaining like auctioneers from hell.

my brothers, the philosophers, they spoke to me unlike
anybody on the streets or anywhere else; they
filled an immense void.
such good boys, ah, such good
boys!

yes, the libraries helped; in my other temple, the
bars, it was another matter, more simplistic, the
language and the way was
different . . .

library days, bar nights.
the nights were alike,
there's some fellow sitting nearby, maybe not a
bad sort, but for me he doesn't shine right,
there's a gruesome deadness there—I think of my father,
of schoolteachers, of faces on coins and bills, of dreams
about murderers with dull eyes; well,

somehow this fellow and I get to exchanging glances,
a fury slowly begins to gather: we are enemies, cat and
dog, priest and atheist, fire and water; tension builds,
block piled upon block, waiting for the crash; our hands
fold and unfold, we drink, now, finally with a
purpose:

his face turns to me:
"sumpin' ya don't like, buddy?"

"yeah. you."

"wanna do sumpin' about it?"

"certainly."

we finish our drinks, rise, move to the back of the
bar, out into the alley; we
turn, face each other.

I say to him, "there's nothing but space between us. you
care to close that
space?"

he rushes toward me and somehow it's a part of the part of the
part.

in and out of the dark

my wife likes movie houses, the popcorn and soft drinks, the
settling into seats, she finds a child's delight in
this and I am happy for her—but really, I myself, I must have
come from another place, I must have been a mole in another
life, something that burrowed and hid alone:
the other people crowded in the seats, near and far, give me
feelings that I dislike; it's stupid, maybe, but there it
is; and then
there's the darkness and then the
giant human faces, bodies, that move about on the screen, they
speak and we
listen.

of one hundred movies there's one that's fair, one that's good
and ninety eight that are very bad.
most movies start badly and steadily get
worse;
if you can believe the actions and speech of the
characters
you might even believe that the popcorn you chew also
has a meaning of
sorts.
(well, it might be that people see so many movies
that when they finally see one not
so bad as the others, they think it's
great. an Academy Award means that you don't stink
quite as much as your cousin.)

the movie ends and we are out in the street, moving
toward the car; "well," says my wife, "it wasn't as
good as they say."
"no," I say, "it wasn't."

"there were a few good parts, though," she replies.
"yeah," I answer.

we are at the car, get in, then I am driving us out
of that part of town; we look around at the night;
the night looks good.

"you hungry?" she asks.

"yes. you?"

we stop at a signal; I watch the red light;
I could eat that red light—anything, anything at
all to fill the void; millions of dollars spent to create
something more terrible than the actual lives of
most living things; one should never have to pay an
admission to hell.

the light changes and we escape,
forward.

be kind

we are always asked
to understand the other person's
viewpoint
no matter how
out-dated
foolish or
obnoxious.

one is asked
to view
their total error
their life-waste
with
kindliness,
especially if they are
aged.

but age is the total of
our doing.
they have aged
badly
because they have
lived
out of focus,
they have refused to
see.

not their fault?

whose fault?
mine?

I am asked to hide
my viewpoint
from them

for fear of their
fear.

age is no crime

but the shame
of a deliberately
wasted
life

among so many
deliberately
wasted
lives

is.

the man with the beautiful eyes

when we were kids
there was a strange house
all the shades were
always
drawn
and we never heard voices
in there
and the yard was full of
bamboo
and we liked to play in
the bamboo
pretend we were
Tarzan
(although there was no
Jane).
and there was a
fish pond
a large one
full of the
fattest goldfish
you ever saw
and they were
tame.
they came to the
surface of the water
and took pieces of
bread
from our hands.

our parents had
told us:
"never go near that
house."
so, of course,
we went.

we wondered if anybody
lived there.
weeks went by and we
never saw
anybody.

then one day
we heard
a voice
from the house
"YOU GOD DAMNED
WHORE!"

it was a man's
voice.

then the screen
door
of the house was
flung open
and the man
walked
out.

he was holding a
fifth of whiskey
in his right
hand.
he was about
30.
he had a cigar
in his
mouth,
needed a
shave.
his hair was
wild and
uncombed
and he was
barefoot

in undershirt
and pants.
but his eyes
were
bright.
they *blazed*
with
brightness
and he said,
"hey, little
gentlemen,
having a good
time, I
hope?"

then he gave a
little laugh
and walked
back into the
house.

we left,
went back to my
parents' yard
and thought
about it.

our parents,
we decided,
had wanted us
to stay away
from there
because they
never wanted us
to see a man
like
that,
a strong natural
man
with

beautiful
eyes.

our parents
were ashamed
that they were
not
like that
man,
that's why they
wanted us
to stay
away.

but
we went back
to that house
and the bamboo
and the tame
goldfish.
we went back
many times
for many
weeks
but we never
saw
or heard
the man
again.

the shades were
down
as always
and it was
quiet.

then one day
as we came back from
school

we saw the
house.

it had burned
down,
there was nothing
left,
just a smoldering
twisted black
foundation
and we went to
the fish pond
and there was
no water
in it
and the fat
orange goldfish
were dead
there,
drying out.

we went back to
my parents' yard
and talked about
it
and decided that
our parents had
burned their
house down,
had killed
them
had killed the
goldfish
because it was
all too
beautiful,
even the bamboo
forest had
burned.

they had been
afraid of
the man with the
beautiful
eyes.

and
we were afraid
then
that
all throughout our lives
things like that
would
happen,
that nobody
wanted
anybody
to be
strong and
beautiful
like that,
that
others would never
allow it,
and that
many people
would have to
die.

a strange day

it was one of those hot and tiring days at Hollywood
Park
with a huge crowd, a
tiring, rude, dumb
crowd.

I won the last race and stayed to collect and when I
got to my car
there was a massive jam of traffic attempting to
work its way out of there.

so I took my shoes off, sat and waited, turned on the
radio, lucked onto some classical music, found
a pint of Scotch in the glove compartment, un-
capped it, had a
hit.

I'm going to let them all get out of here, I
thought, then I'll
go.

I found ¾'s of a cigar, lit it, had another hit
of Scotch.

I listened to the music, smoked, drank the
Scotch and watched the losers
leave.

there was even a little crap game going
about 100 yards to the
east

then that
broke up.

I decided to finish the
pint.

I did, then stretched out on the
seat.

I don't know how long I
slept
but when I awakened it was dark and
the parking lot was
empty.

I decided not to put on my shoes, started the car
and drove out of
there. . . .

when I got back to my place I could hear the phone
ringing.

as I put the key in the door and opened it,
the phone kept
ringing.

I walked over, picked up the
phone.

"hello?"

"you son of a bitch, where have you
been?"

"the racetrack."

"the racetrack? it's 12:30 a.m.! I've been
phoning since
7 p.m.!"

"I just got in from the
racetrack."

"you got some woman
there?"

"no."

"I don't believe you!"
she hung up.

I walked to the refrigerator, got a beer, went to
the bathroom, let the water run in the
tub.
I finished the beer, got another, opened it and
climbed into the
tub.

the phone rang
again.

I got out of the tub with my beer and
dripping away
I walked to the phone, picked it
up.

"hello?"

"you son of a bitch, I still don't
believe you!"

she hung up.

I walked back to the tub with my beer,
leaving another trail of
water.

as I got back into the tub
the phone rang
again.

I let it ring, counting the
rings: 1,2,3,4,5,6,7,8,9,

10,11,12,13,14,15,
16 . . .

she hung up.

then, perhaps, 3 or 4 minutes
passed.

the phone rang
again.

I counted the rings:
1,2,3,4,5,6,7,8,
9 . . .

then it was
quiet.

about then I remembered I had
left my shoes in the
car.
no matter, except I only had
one pair.

chances were, though, that nobody
would ever want to steal that
car.

I got out of the tub for another
beer,
leaving another trail
behind me.

it was the end of a
long
long
day.

Trollius and trellises

of course, I may die in the next ten minutes
and I'm ready for that
but what I'm really worried about is
that my editor-publisher might retire
even though he is ten years younger than
I.
it was just 25 years ago (I was at that *ripe*
old age of 45)
when we began our unholy alliance to
test the literary waters,
neither of us being much
known.

I think we had some luck and still have some
of same
yet
the odds are pretty fair
that he will opt for warm and pleasant
afternoons
in the garden
long before I.

writing is its own intoxication
while publishing and editing,
attempting to collect bills
carries its own
attrition
which also includes dealing with the
petty bitchings and demands
of many
so-called genius darlings who are
not.

I won't blame him for getting
out
and hope he sends me photos of his
Rose Lane, his
Gardenia Avenue.

will I have to seek other
promulgators?
that fellow in the Russian
fur hat?
or that beast in the East
with all that hair
in his ears, with those wet and
greasy lips?

or will my editor-publisher
upon exiting for that world of Trollius and
trellis
hand over the
machinery
of his former trade to a
cousin, a
daughter or
some Poundian from Big
Sur?

or will he just pass the legacy on
to the
Shipping Clerk
who will rise like
Lazarus,
fingering new-found
importance?

one can imagine terrible
things:
"Mr. Chinaski, all your work
must now be submitted in
Rondo form
and
typed
triple-spaced on rice
paper."

power corrupts,
life aborts

and all you
have left
is a
bunch of
warts.

"no, no, Mr. Chinaski:
Rondo form!"

"hey, man," I'll ask,
"haven't you heard of
the thirties?"

"the thirties? what's
that?"

my present editor-publisher
and I
at times
did discuss the thirties,
the Depression
and
some of the little tricks it
taught us—
like how to endure on almost
nothing
and move forward
anyhow.

well, John, if it happens enjoy your
divertissement to
plant husbandry,
cultivate and aerate
between
bushes, water only in the
early morning, spread
shredding to discourage
weed growth
and
as I do in my writing:

use plenty of
manure.

and thank you
for locating me there at
5124 DeLongpre Avenue
somewhere between
alcoholism and
madness.

together we
laid down the gauntlet
and there are takers
even at this late date
still to be
found
as the fire sings
through the
trees.

air and light and time and space

"—you know, I've either had a family, a job, something
has always been in the
way
but now
I've sold my house, I've found this
place, a large studio, you should see the *space* and
the *light*.
for the first time in my life I'm going to have a place and the time to
create."

no baby, if you're going to create
you're going to create whether you work
16 hours a day in a coal mine
or
you're going to create in a small room with 3 children
while you're on
welfare,
you're going to create with part of your mind and your
body blown
away,
you're going to create blind
crippled
demented,
you're going to create with a cat crawling up your
back while
the whole city trembles in earthquake, bombardment,
flood and fire.

baby, air and light and time and space
have nothing to do with it
and don't create anything
except maybe a longer life to find
new excuses
for.

the eagle of the heart—

what will they be writing about 2,000 years from
now
if they are
here?

now
I drink cabernet sauvignon while
listening to
Bach: it's
most curious: this
continuing death
            this
continuing life

as
I look at this hand
holding a cigarette
I feel as if
I have been here
forever.

now
troops with bayonets
sack
the town below.
my dog, Tony, smiles at
me.

it is well
to feel good
for no reason;
or
with a limited
choice to
choose
anyhow;
or with a little love,

not to buckle to
hatred.
faith, brother, not in the
gods
but in
yourself:
don't ask,
tell.

I tell you
such fine
music
waits
in the
shadows
of
hell.

bright red car

I try to avoid speed duels on the freeway but the most curious thing
is
that all my speeding tickets are when I am quietly driving along on
my
own.

when I am in a high speed duel, darting in and out of lanes
at near 100 m.p.h.
the police are never
about.

when I get tagged for speeding it is for cruising along,
day-dreaming, at a mere 70
m.p.h.

I received 3 such nonsensical tickets in 3 weeks so
I laid low for some time—2 years, in fact, but today
out there
there was a fellow in a bright red car, I have no idea what
model or kind
and I have no idea of how it all started but I believe that
I started it:
I was in the fast lane going about 70
and I caught the flash of bright red in my rear view and
as he swung out to pass me on the right
he was doing 75
and there was time for him to pass
then cut into the fast lane ahead of me
but *something* made me hit the throttle and cut him
off
locking him in behind an old lady with a CHRIST
SAVES bumper sticker.
this seemed to piss him no end
and next I knew he had swung over on my bumper,
so close that his windshield and my taillights
seemed one.

this pissed *me* no end and I was being blocked by a
green Volks directly ahead
but I cut right through an opening and shot
ahead.
bright red went wild, spotted the far lane open,
roared over and gunned it
along.

after that, it was just me and bright red
jockeying for spots.

he would garner a lead, then with a crazy gamble
of lane change I would regain the
lead.

during this duel my destination was forgotten and I'm
        sure his was
too.

watching him, I couldn't help but admire his driving
skill; he took a few more chances than I
but I had a little bit the better machine
so it
just about evened out.

then
suddenly
we were alone: a freak break in the traffic
had set us free together
and we really opened
up.

he had a short lead but my machine slowly gained; I
inched up near him,
then I was at his side and I couldn't help but
look over.

he was a young Japanese-American, maybe 18, 19
and I looked at him and
laughed.

I saw him check me out.
he saw a 70 year old white man
with a face like
Frankenstein.

the young man took his foot off the throttle and
dropped back.

I let him go.

I turned the radio
on.

I was 18 miles past my destination but it
didn't matter.

it was a beautiful sunny day.

moving toward the 21st century

it was a New Year's Eve party at my place
I think.
I was standing   holding a drink   when
this slender young fellow   walked up
he was a bit drunk   he said

"Hank, I met a woman who said
she was married to you for 2
years."

"really?
what was her
name?"

"Lola
Edwards."

"never heard of
her."

"ah, come on, man, she
said . . ."

"don't know her,
baby . . ."

in fact   I didn't know   who
he was . . .

I drained my drink   walked to the kitchen
poured a refill

I looked around   yes, I was at my place
I recognized the
kitchen.

another
Happy New Year.

Jesus.

I walked out to face the
people.

the lady and the mountain lion

it was hardly a wilderness area
but it was countryside
and there had been a paucity of
rainfall—also some housing
construction on the
hillsides.

small game was dying
out.
the coyotes were the first of
the famished to
arrive
looking for
chickens
cats
anything.

in fact, a group attacked
a man on horseback
tearing his arm
but he
escaped.

then
in a park
there was the lady who
left her car to
go to the public
restroom.

she had closed the stall
door
when she heard a
soft
sound,
the stealth of

padded
feet.

then
as she sat there
the mountain lion stuck
his head under the
stall door.

a truly beautiful
animal.

then
the head withdrew, the cat
knocked over a trash can, circled,
emitted a slow
growl.

the lady climbed up
on the toilet
then grasped an overhead
pipe
and
swung herself completely up
(fear creates abnormal
acts) and sat where
she could watch
the cat.

at once
the cat put his
paws up
on the wash basin
stuck his head in
there
and lapped at a dripping
spigot.

then
he sank

low upon the floor
crouched
facing the doorway

then
zing
was gone
out of there.

then
at last
the lady began
screaming.

when the people
arrived
the cat was nowhere to be
seen.

the story made the
newspapers and the television
stations.

the story that won't be told is
that the lady
will never go to the bathroom
again
without thinking of a
mountain
lion.

a truly beautiful
animal.

a laugh a minute

come on, let's go see him, this old guy is a
kick in the ass, 50 years old, he sits around
in his shorts and underwear
drinking wine out of this chipped white
cup.
he sits with the shades pulled down and
he's never owned a tv set.
the only time he goes out is for more
wine
or to the racetrack in his baby blue
'58 Comet.

you get there and he's distraught, some woman
has always left forever and
he pretends to play it with bravado but
his little slit eyes are filled with
pain.

he'll pour drinks all around, he just gulps
that crap down and then sometimes he'll
get up and puke.
it's really something. you
can hear him for blocks.
then he'll come out and pour another
drink.
he'll go on and on drinking
and then once in a while he'll say something
crazy like, "anything 3 dogs can do, 4 dogs
can do better!"
other things too.
or he'll smash a glass or a bottle against
the wall.

he worked as an orderly in a
hospital for 15 years
then quit.

he never sleeps at night.

and for a guy that ugly
I don't see how he gets all his
women.
and he's jealous.
just look at one of his women
and he'll swing on you.

then he gets drunk and tells crazy
stories and sings.
and guess what? he writes
poetry.

come on, let's go see him, this old guy
is a kick in the
ass!

hello, Hamsun

after two-and-one-half bottles
that have not strengthened my saddened
heart

walking from this drunken
darkness
toward the bedroom
thinking of Hamsun who
ate his own flesh to
gain time to
write

I trundle into the other
room
an old
man

a hellfish in the night
swimming upward
sideways
down.

death is smoking my cigars

you know: I'm drunk once again
here
listening to Tchaikovsky
on the radio.
Jesus, I heard him 47 years
ago
when I was a starving writer
and here he is
again
and now I am a minor success as
a writer
and death is walking
up and down
this room
smoking my cigars
taking hits of my
wine
as Tchaik is working away
at the *Pathétique,*
it's been some journey
and any luck I've had was
because I rolled the dice
right:
I starved for my art, I starved to
gain 5 god-damned minutes, 5 hours,
5 days—
I just wanted to get the word
down;
fame, money, didn't matter:
I wanted the word down
and *they* wanted me at a punch press,
a factory assembly line
they wanted me to be a stock boy in a
department store.

well, death says, as he walks by,
I'm going to get you anyhow

no matter what you've been:
writer, cab-driver, pimp, butcher,
sky-diver, I'm going to get
you . . .

o.k. baby, I tell him.

we drink together now
as one a.m. slides to 2
a.m. and
only he knows the
moment, but I worked a con
on him: I got my
5 god-damned minutes
and much
more.

hock shops

were always all right with me
because when I tried to sell something in the street
there were no takers.

of course, the shops offered far less than real value;
they had to profit on the
resale,
but at least, they were
there.

my favorite shop was a place in Los Angeles—
this fellow would lead me to a booth where
he would gather a black curtain all around
us,
it slid on little rings
and then
we would be enclosed.

and it always went like
this:

"show me," he would
say.

I would place the item on the table under
the very strong
light.

he would examine the item, then look at me
for some time.

"I can't give you very much for
this."

another pause, then he would name his
price.

the offer was always more than I
expected.

"I'll take $10," I would name a
higher price.

"no," he would answer, "in fact . . ."
and then he would mention a lower price
than his original
offer.

at times I would attempt to joke with
him:

"if I stay here long enough, I'll be
paying *you* . . ."

he wouldn't smile.

"we don't have to do business at
all."

"listen, I'll accept your *first*
offer . . ."

"very well," he would say,
"but I will *lose* on
this . . ."

then he would write out the
pawn ticket and give me the
money.

"please be sure to read your ticket,
there are
stipulations."

then he would turn off the light
and pull the black curtain
away . . .

sometimes I was able to retrieve one
of the items
but eventually they all returned
forever.

also, I found out that the one thing
you *could* sell in the bars and on the
street were
hock shop tickets.

the hock shops helped me through some terrible
times and I was glad they were
there when nothing else
was, and that booth with the black
curtain: what a marvelous sanctuary,
a place to give up something for
something else that you needed
much more.

how many typewriters, suits, gloves and
watches I left in the hock shops
I have no
idea,
but those places were always
all right
with me.

hell is a closed door

even when starving
the rejection slips hardly ever bothered me:
I only believed that the editors were
truly stupid
and I just went on and wrote more and
more.
I even considered rejects as
action; the worst was the empty
mailbox.

if I had a weakness or a dream
it was
that I only wanted to *see* one of these
editors
who rejected me,
to *see* his or her face, the way they
dressed, the way they walked across a
room, the sound of their voice, the look
in their eye . . .
just *one* look at *one* of
them—

you see, when all you look at is
a piece of printed paper
telling you that you
aren't very good,
then there is a tendency
to think that the editors
are more god-like than
they are.

hell is a closed door
when you're starving for your god-
damned art
but sometimes you feel at least like having a
peek through the
keyhole.

young or old, good or bad,
I don't think anything dies as slow and
as hard as a
writer.

pulled down shade

what I like about you
she told me
is that you're crude—
look at you sitting there
a beercan in your hand
and a cigar in your mouth
and look at
your dirty hairy belly
sticking out from
under your shirt.
you've got your shoes off
and you've got a hole
in your right stocking
with the big toe
sticking out.
you haven't shaved in
4 or 5 days.
your teeth are yellow
and your eyebrows
hang down
all twisted
and you've got enough
scars
to scare the shit
out of anybody.
there's always
a ring
in your bathtub
your telephone
is covered with
grease
and
half the crap in
your refrigerator is
rotten.
you never
wash your car.

you've got newspapers
a week old
on the floor.
you read dirty
magazines
and you don't have
a tv
but you order
deliveries from the
liquor store
and you tip
good.
and best of all
you don't push
a woman to
go to bed
with you.
you seem hardly
interested
and when I talk to you
you don't
say anything
you just
look around
the room or
scratch your
neck
like you don't
hear me.
you've got an old
wet towel in
the sink
and a photo of
Mussolini
on the wall
and you never
complain
about anything
and you never
ask questions

and I've
known you for
6 months
but I have
no idea
who you are.
you're like
some
pulled down shade
but that's what
I like about
you:
your crudeness:
a woman can
drop
out of your
life and
forget you
real fast.
a woman
can't go anywhere
but UP
after
leaving you,
honey.
you've got to
be
the best thing
that ever
happened
to
a girl
who's between
one guy
and the next
and has nothing
to do
at the moment.
this fucking

Scotch is
great.
let's play
Scrabble.

before Aids

I'm glad I got to them
all, I'm glad I got so many of them
in.

I flipped them
poked them
gored them.

so many high-heeled shoes
under my bed
it looked like a January
Clearance Sale.

the cheap hotel rooms,
the drunken fights,
the phones ringing,
the walls banging

I was
wild
red-eyed
big-balled
unshaven
poor
foul-mouthed
I laughed
plenty

and I picked them off
the barstools
like
ripe plums.

dirty sheets
bad whiskey
bad breath
cheap cigars

and to hell with the next
morning.

I always slept with my
wallet under my
pillow
bedded down with the
depressed and the
crazies.

I was barred from half the
hotels in
Los Angeles.

I'm glad I got to them all,
I plugged and banged and
sang and
some of them
sang with me
on those glorious
3 a.m. mornings.
when the cops
arrived, that was
grand,
we barricaded the doors
and taunted
them
and they never waited around
until noon
(checking-out time) to
arrest us,
we weren't that
important

but
I thought we were
walking toward the bar,
and what a place the bar was
around noon, so quiet and
empty,

a place to begin
again,
to buck up with a quiet
beer,
looking out across at the
park
with the ducks over there
and the tall trees
over there.

so,
always broke but always
money from somewhere,
I waited
getting ready to
plug and bang and poke
and sing again
in those good old times
in those very very very
good old times
before Aids.

hunk of rock

Nina was the hardest of them
all,
the worst woman I had known
up to that moment
and I was sitting in front of
my secondhand black and white
tv
watching the news
when I heard a suspicious
sound in the kitchen
and I ran out there
and saw her with
a full bottle of whiskey—
a 5th—
and she had it and
was headed for the back porch
door
but I caught her and
grabbed at the bottle.
"give me that bottle, you
fucking whore!"
and we wrestled for the
bottle
and let me tell you
she gave me a good fight
for it
but
I got it away from her
and I told her to
get her ass out of
there.
she lived in the same place
in the back
upstairs.

I locked the door
took the bottle and a

glass
went out to the couch
sat down and
opened the bottle and
poured myself a good
one.

I shut off the tv and
sat there
thinking about what a
hard number
Nina was.
I came up with
at least
a dozen lousy things
she had done
to me.

what a whore.
what a hunk of rock.

I sat there drinking
the whiskey
and wondering
what I was doing
with Nina.

then there was a
knock on the
door.
it was Nina's friend,
Helga.

"where's Nina?"
she asked.

"she tried to steal
my whiskey, I
ran her ass
out of here."

"she said to meet
her here."

"what for?"

"she said me and her
were going to do it
in front of you
for $50."

"$25."

"she said $50."

"well, she's not
here . . . want a
drink?"

"sure . . ."

I got Helga a glass
poured her a
whiskey.
she took a
hit.

"maybe," she said,
"I ought to go get
Nina."

"I don't want to see
her."

"why not?"

"she's a whore."

Helga finished her
drink and I poured
her another.

she took a
hit.

"Benny calls me a
whore, I'm no
whore."

Benny was the guy
she was shacked
with.

"I know you're no
whore, Helga."

"thanks. Ain't ya got no
music?"

"just the radio . . ."

she saw it
got up
turned it
on.
some music came
blaring out.

Helga began to
dance
holding her whiskey
glass in one
hand.
she wasn't a good
dancer
she looked
ridiculous.

she stopped
drained her drink
rolled her glass along the
rug

then ran toward
me
dropped to her knees
unzipped me
and then
she was down
there
doing tricks.

I drained my
drink
poured another.

she was
good.
she had a college
degree
some place back
East.

"get it, Helga, get
it!"

there was a loud
knock
on the front
door.

"HANK, IS HELGA
THERE?"

"WHO?"

"HELGA!"

"JUST A MINUTE!"

"THIS IS NINA, I WAS
SUPPOSED TO MEET
HELGA HERE, WE HAVE A

LITTLE SURPRISE FOR
YOU!"

"YOU TRIED TO STEAL
MY WHISKEY, YOU
WHORE!"

"HANK, LET ME
IN!"

"get it, Helga, get
it!"

"HANK!"

"Helga, you fucking whore . . .
Helga! Helga! Helga!!"

I pulled away and
got up.

"let her in."

I went to the
bathroom.

when I came out they
were both sitting there
drinking and smoking
laughing about
something.
then they
saw me.

"50 bucks," said Nina.

"25 bucks," I said.

"we won't do it
then."

"don't then."

Nina inhaled
exhaled.
"all right, you
cheap bastard, 25
bucks!"

Nina stood up and
began taking her
clothes off.

she was the hardest
of them
all.

Helga stood up and
began taking her
clothes off.

I poured a
drink.
"sometimes I wonder
what the hell is
going on
around here," I
said.

"don't worry about
it, Daddy, just
get with it!"

"just what am I
supposed to
do?"

"just do
whatever the fuck
you feel
like doing,"
said Nina
her big ass
blazing
in the
lamplight.

poetry

it
takes
a lot of

desperation

dissatisfaction

and
disillusion

to
write

a
few
good
poems.

it's not
for
everybody

either to

write
it

or even to

read
it.

dinner, 1933

when my father ate
his lips became
greasy
with food.

and when he ate
he talked about how
good
the food was
and that
most other people
didn't eat
as good
as we
did.

he liked to
sop up
what was left
on his plate
with a piece of
bread,
meanwhile making
appreciative sounds
rather like
half-
grunts.

he *slurped* his
coffee
making loud
bubbling
sounds.
then he'd put
the cup
down:

"dessert? is it
jello?"

my mother would
bring it
in a large bowl
and my father would
spoon it
out.

as it plopped
in the dish
the jello made
strange sounds,
almost fart-
like
sounds.

then came the
whipped cream,
mounds of it
on the
jello.

"ah! jello and
whipped cream!"

my father sucked the
jello and whipped
cream
off his spoon—
it sounded as if it
was entering a
wind
tunnel.

finished with
that
he would wipe his
mouth

with a huge white
napkin,
rubbing hard
in circular
motions,
the napkin almost
hiding his
entire
face.

after that
out came the
Camel
cigarettes.
he'd light one
with a wooden
kitchen match,
then place the
match,
still burning,
onto an
ashtray.

then a slurp of
coffee, the cup
back down, and a good
drag on the
Camel.

"ah that was a
good
meal!"

moments later
in my bedroom
on my bed
in the dark
the food that I
had eaten
and what I had

seen
was already
making me
ill.

the only good
thing
was
listening to
the crickets
out there,
out there
in another world
I didn't
live
in.

such luck

we were at this table,
men and women,
after dinner.
somehow
the conversation got
around to
PMS.
one of the ladies
stated firmly that
the only cure for
PMS
was old
age.
there were other
remarks
that I have
forgotten,
except for one
which came from this
German guest
once married,
now divorced.
also, I had seen
him with
any number of
beautiful young
girlfriends.
anyhow, after quietly
listening
to our conversation
for some time
he asked us,
"what's PMS?"

now here was one
truly touched

by
the angels.

the light was so
bright
we
all looked
away.

flophouse

you haven't lived
until you've been in a
flophouse
with nothing but one
light bulb
and 56 men
squeezed together
on cots
with everybody
snoring
at once
and some of those
snores
so
deep and
gross and
unbelievable—
dark
snotty
gross
subhuman
wheezings
from hell
itself.

your mind
almost breaks
under those
death-like
sounds

and the
intermingling
odors:
hard
unwashed socks
pissed and

shitted
underwear

and over it all
slowly circulating
air
much like that
emanating from
uncovered
garbage
cans.

and those
bodies
in the dark

fat and
thin
and
bent

some
legless
armless

some
mindless

and worst of
all:
the total
absence of
hope

it shrouds
them
covers them
totally.

it's not
bearable.

you get
up

go out

walk the
streets

up and
down
sidewalks

past buildings

around the
corner

and back
up
the same
street

thinking

those men
were all
children
once

what has happened
to
them?

and what has
happened
to
me?

it's dark
and cold
out
here.

hand-outs

sometimes I am hit
for change
3 or 4 times
in twenty minutes
and nine times out of
ten I'll
give.
the time or two
that I don't
I have an instinctive
reaction
not to
and I
don't
but mostly I
dig and
give
but each time
I can't help but
remember
the many times
hollow-eyed
my skin tight to the
ribs
my mind airy and
mad
I never asked
anybody
for anything
and it wasn't
pride
it was simply because
I didn't respect
them
didn't regard them
as worthy human
beings.

they were the
enemy
and they still are
as I dig
in
and
give.

waiting

hot summers in the mid-30's in Los Angeles
where every 3rd lot was vacant
and it was a short ride to the orange
groves—
if you had a car and the
gas.

hot summers in the mid-30's in Los Angeles
too young to be a man and too old to
be a boy.

hard times.
a neighbor tried to rob our
house, my father caught him
climbing through the
window,
held him there in the dark
on the floor:
"you rotten son of a
bitch!"

"Henry, Henry, let me go,
let me go!"

"you son of a bitch, I'll kill
you!"

my mother phoned the police.

another neighbor set his house on fire
in an attempt to collect the
insurance.
he was investigated and
jailed.

hot summers in the mid-30's in Los Angeles,
nothing to do, nowhere to go, listening to

the terrified talk of our parents
at night:
"what will we do? what will we
do?"

"god, I don't know . . ."

starving dogs in the alleys, skin taut
across ribs, hair falling out, tongues
out, such sad eyes, sadder than any sadness
on earth.

hot summers in the mid-30's in Los Angeles,
the men of the neighborhood were quiet
and the women were like pale
statues.

the parks full of socialists,
communists, anarchists, standing on the park
benches, orating, agitating.

the sun came down through a clear sky and
the ocean was clean
and we were
neither men nor
boys.

we fed the dogs leftover pieces of dry hard
bread
which they ate gratefully,
eyes shining in
wonder,
tails waving at such
luck

as
World War II moved toward us,
even then, during those
hot summers in the mid-30's in Los Angeles.

those mornings

I still remember those New Orleans rats
out on the balcony railings
in the dark of early morning
as I stood waiting my turn at the
crapper.
there were always two or three
big ones
just sitting there—sometimes they'd
move quickly then
stop and sit there.
I looked at them and they looked at
me.
they showed no fear.

at last the crapper door would open
and out would walk
one of the tenants
and he always looked worse than
the rats
and then he'd be gone
down the hallway
and I'd go into the still-
stinking crapper
with my hangover.

and almost always
when I came out
the rats would be gone.
as soon as it got a little light
they would
vanish.

and then
the world would be
mine,
I'd walk down the stairway
and into it

and my low-wage
pitiful
job
while remembering the
rats,
how it was better for them
than for
me.

I walked to work as the sun
came up hot
and the whores slept
like
babies.

everything you touch

putting on your torn clothes in an old New Orleans roominghouse,
you and your stockboy soul,
then rolling your little green wagon past the salesgirls who
took no notice of you, those girls dreaming of bigger
game with their tiny rectangular
brains.

or in Los Angeles, coming in from your shipping clerk job at
an auto parts warehouse, taking the elevator up to 319 to find
your woman sprawled out on the bed, drunk at
6 p.m.

you were never any good at picking them, you always got the
leftovers, the crazies, the alkies, the pill-freaks.
maybe that was all you could get and maybe you were all they
could get.

you went to the bars and found more alkies, pill-freaks, crazies.
all they had to show you were a pair of well-turned ankles in
spike-heeled shoes.
you thumped up and down on beds with them as if you had
        discovered
the meaning of
existence.

then there was this day at work when Larry the salesman came
        down the
aisle with his big belly and his little button eyes, Larry always
walked loudly on leather-soled shoes and he was almost always
whistling.

he stopped whistling and stood at your shipping table as you
worked.

then he began rocking back and forth, he had this habit and
he stood there rocking, observing you, he was one of those jokers,
        you

know, and then he began laughing, you were sick from a long crazy
night, needed a shave, you were dressed in a torn shirt.

"what is it, Larry?" you asked.

and then he said, "Hank, everything you touch turns to shit!"

you couldn't argue with him about that.

car wash

got out, fellow said, "hey!" walked toward
me, we shook hands, he slipped me 2 red
tickets for free car washes, "find you later,"
I told him, walked on through to waiting
area with wife, we sat on outside bench.
black fellow with a limp came up, said,
"hey, man, how's it going?"
I answered, "fine, bro, you makin' it?"
"no problem," he said, then walked off to
dry down a Caddy.
"these people know you?" my wife asked.
"no."
"how come they talk to you?"
"they like me, people have always liked me,
it's my cross."
then our car was finished, fellow flipped
his rag at me, we got up, got to the
car, I slipped him a buck, we got in, I
started the engine, the foreman walked
up, big guy with dark shades, huge guy,
he smiled a big one, "good to see you,
man!"
I smiled back, "thanks, but it's your party,
man!"
I pulled out into traffic, "they know you,"
said my wife.
"sure," I said, "I've been there."

the flashing of the odds

parking lot attendant, Bobby, was funny,
wise-cracking, laughing, was
good at it, he was an original,
sometimes when I was down
listening to Bobby brought me back
up.

didn't see him for 3 weeks, asked the
other attendants but they didn't know
or made things up.

drove in today and there was
Bobby, his uniform wrinkled, he was just
standing there while the others
worked.

approached him and he seemed to
recognize me, then spoke: "got all
stressed out driving here, it took me
3 hours!"

he wasn't laughing, had grown suddenly
fat, his belt buckle was
unfastened, I buckled him up, he
had a 3 day beard,
his
hair was grey, his face wrinkled, his
eyes stuck in a backwash, 20 years
lost in 3 weeks.

"good to see you, Bobby."

"yeah, sure, when you going to buy
this place?"

he was talking about the
racetrack.

I walked across the lot and into
the track, took the escalator
up, reached the top floor, walked
toward the service stand.
Betty saw me and got my coffee
poured.

"you ready for a big day?"
she asked.

"I'm ready for any kind of
day."

"you come here to win, don't
you?"

"I come here not to
lose."

I took my coffee to a seat
facing the toteboard.
the odds flashed, I sat down
spilling hot coffee
on my
hand.

"shit," I said.

and the day went
on.

poetry contest

send as many poems as you wish, only
keep each to a maximum of ten lines.
no limit as to style or content
although we prefer poems of
affirmation.
double space
with your name and address in the
upper left hand
corner.
editors not responsible for
manuscripts
without an s.a.s.e.
every effort
will be made to
judge all works within 90
days.
after careful screening
the final choices will be made by
Elly May Moody,
general editor in charge.
please enclose ten dollars for
each poem
submitted.
a final grand prize of
seventy-five dollars will
be awarded the winner
of the
*Elly May Moody Golden Poetry
Award,*
along with a scroll
signed by
Elly May Moody.
there will also be 2nd, 3rd and
4th prize scrolls
also signed by
Elly May Moody.
all decisions will be

final.
the prize winners will
appear in the Spring issue of
The Heart of Heaven.
prize winners will also receive
one copy of the magazine
along with
Elly May Moody's
latest collection of
poetry,
*The Place Where Winter
Died.*

peace

near the corner table in the
cafe
a middle-aged couple
sit.
they have finished their
meal
and they are each drinking a
beer.
it is 9 in the evening.
she is smoking a
cigarette.
then he says something.
she nods.
then she speaks.
he grins, moves his
hand.
then they are
quiet.
through the blinds next to
their table
flashing red neon
blinks on and
off.

there is no war.
there is no hell.

then he raises his beer
bottle.
it is green.
he lifts it to his lips,
tilts it.

it is a coronet.

her right elbow is
on the table

and in her hand
she holds the
cigarette
between her thumb and
forefinger
and
as she watches
him
the streets outside
flower
in the
night.

the bluebird

there's a bluebird in my heart that
wants to get out
but I'm too tough for him,
I say, stay in there, I'm not going
to let anybody see
you.

there's a bluebird in my heart that
wants to get out
but I pour whiskey on him and inhale
cigarette smoke
and the whores and the bartenders
and the grocery clerks
never know that
he's
in there.

there's a bluebird in my heart that
wants to get out
but I'm too tough for him,
I say,
stay down, do you want to mess
me up?
you want to screw up the
works?
you want to blow my book sales in
Europe?

there's a bluebird in my heart that
wants to get out
but I'm too clever, I only let him out
at night sometimes
when everybody's asleep.
I say, I know that you're there,
so don't be
sad.

then I put him back,
but he's singing a little
in there, I haven't quite let him
die
and we sleep together like
that
with our
secret pact
and it's nice enough to
make a man
weep, but I don't
weep, do
you?

2

*living too long
takes more than
time*

going out

the sweet slide of the luger
toward your temple,
a flight of birds winging
northward,
the clicking sound of the
safety catch being
released,
the eclipse of the
sun,
the sound of something being
shut
hard,
pal.

the replacements

Jack London drinking his life away while
writing of strange and heroic men.
Eugene O'Neill drinking himself oblivious
while writing his dark and poetic
works.

now our moderns
lecture at universities
in tie and suit,
the little boys soberly studious,
the little girls with glazed eyes
looking
up,
the lawns so green, the books so dull,
the life so dying of
thirst.

the genius

this man sometimes forgets who
he is.
sometimes he thinks he's the
Pope.

other times he thinks he's a
hunted rabbit
and hides under the
bed.

then
all at once
he'll recapture total
clarity
and begin creating
works of
art.

then he'll be all right
for some
time.

then, say,
he'll be sitting with his
wife
and 3 or 4 other
people
discussing various
matters

he will be charming,
incisive,
original.

then he'll do
something
strange.

like once
he stood up
unzipped
and began
pissing
on the
rug.

another time
he ate a paper
napkin.

and there was
the time
he got into his
car
and drove it
backwards
all the way to
the
grocery store
and back
again
backwards
the other motorists
screaming at
him
but he
made it
there and
back
without
incident
and without
being
stopped
by a patrol
car.

but he's best
as the
Pope
and his
Latin
is very
good.

his works of
art
aren't that
exceptional
but they allow him
to
survive
and to live with
a series of
19-year-old
wives
who
cut his hair
his toenails
bib
tuck and
feed
him.

he wears everybody
out
but
himself.

a poet in New York

eating out tonight
I find a table alone
and while waiting for my order
take out my wife's copy of
A Poet in New York.
I often carry things to read
so that I will not have to look at
the people.

I find the poems bad (for me)
these poems written in 1929
the year of the stock market
crash.

I close the book and look at
the people.

my order arrives.
the food is bad too.

some say that bad and good
run in streaks.

I hope so.
I wait for the good, put a slice of
lemon chicken into my
mouth, chew
and pretend that everything is
fairly
fine.

no sale

I just sat in the bar
non compos mentis.

it was about a week before
Xmas.
big Ed was selling trees
outside.

he came into the
bar.

"Jesus, it's freezing out
there!"

big Ed looked at me.

"Hank, you go stand out there
with the trees.
if anybody wants to buy
one, you come in and
get me."

I stood outside.

I was in my shirt sleeves.
I didn't have a coat.
it was snowing.
it was ice cold
but a nice ice
cold.
I wasn't used to snow
but I liked the snow.

I stood with the trees.

I stood there about 20
minutes

then big Ed came
out.

"nobody come by?"

"no, Ed."

"you go on in, tell Billy Boy
to give you a drink on
my tab."

I walked in
got a stool.

I told Billy Boy,
"double scotch and water,
Ed's tab."

Billy Boy poured.

"you sell any trees?"

"no trees."

Billy Boy looked at
the patrons.

"hey, Hank didn't sell
no trees."

"whatsa matter, Hank?"
somebody asked.

I didn't answer.
I took a hit of my
drink.

"how come no trees were
sold?" somebody else
asked.

"as the bee swarms to
honey, as night follows
day
in the stink of time,
it will
happen."

"what will happen?"

"somebody will sell a tree
though it won't necessarily
be me."

I finished my drink.

there was
silence.

then somebody said,
"this guy is some kind of
nut."

being there
with those
I decided
I had no argument
with
that.

this

self-congratulatory nonsense as the
famous gather to applaud their seeming
greatness

you
wonder where
the real ones are

what
giant cave
hides them

as
the deathly talentless
bow to
accolades

as
the fools are
fooled
again

you
wonder where
the real ones are

if there are
real ones.

this
self-congratulatory nonsense
has lasted
decades
and
with some exceptions

centuries.

this
is so dreary
is so absolutely pitiless

it
churns the gut to
powder
shackles hope

it
makes little things
like
pulling up a shade
or
putting on your shoes
or
walking out on the street

more difficult
near
damnable

as
the famous gather to
applaud their
seeming
greatness

as
the fools are
fooled
again

humanity
you sick
motherfucker.

now

to reach here
gliding into old age
the decades gone
without ever meeting one person
truly evil
without ever meeting one person
truly exceptional
without ever meeting one person
truly good

gliding into old age

the decades gone

the mornings are the worst.

in error

a warrior
I come in from a long but
victorious day
at the track.

she greets me with some
trash
which I carry and dump
into the garbage
can.

"Jesus Christ," she says,
"push the lid down tight!
the ants will be
everywhere!"

I push the lid down tight.

I think of Amsterdam.
I think of pigeons flying from a
roof.
I think of Time dangling from
a
paper clip.

she's right, of course: the lid
should be
tight.

I walk slowly back
into
the
house.

confession

waiting for death
like a cat
that will jump on the
bed

I am so very sorry for
my wife

she will see this
stiff
white
body

shake it once, then
maybe
again:

"Hank!"

Hank won't
answer.

it's not my death that
worries me, it's my wife
left with this
pile of
nothing.

I want to
let her know
though
that all the nights
sleeping
beside her

even the useless
arguments
were things

ever splendid

and the hard
words
I ever feared to
say
can now be
said:

I love
you.

mugged

finished,
can't find the handle,
mugged in the backalleys of nowhere,
too many dark days and nights,
too many unkind noons, plus a
steady fixation for
the ladies of death.

I am
finished. roll me
up, package
me,
toss me
to the birds of Normandy or the
gulls of Santa Monica, I
no longer
read
I
no longer
breed,
I
talk to old men over quiet
fences.

is this where my suicide complex
un-
complexes?: as
I am asked over the telephone:
did you ever know Kerouac?

I now allow cars to pass me on the freeway.
I haven't been in a fist fight for 15 years.
I have to get up and piss 3 times a night.

and when I see a sexpot on the street I
only see
trouble.

I am
finished, back to square one,
drinking alone and listening to classical
music.

much about dying is getting ready.
the tiger walks through my dreams.

the cigarette in my mouth just exploded.

curious things still do
occur.

no, I never knew Kerouac.

so you see:
my life wasn't
useless
after
all.

the writer

when I think of the things I endured trying to be a
writer—all those rooms in all those cities,
nibbling on tiny bits of food that wouldn't
keep a rat
alive.

I was so thin I could slice bread with my
shoulderblades, only I seldom had
bread . . .
meanwhile, writing things down
again and again
on pieces of paper.

and when I moved from one place to
another
my cardboard suitcase was just
that: paper outside stuffed with
paper inside.

each new landlady would
ask, "what do you
do?"

"I'm a writer."

"oh . . ."

as I settled into tiny rooms to evoke my
craft
many of them pitied me, gave me little
tidbits like apples, walnuts,
peaches . . .
little did they know
that that
was about all that I
ate.

but their pity ended when
they found cheap wine bottles in my
place.

it's all right to be a starving writer
but not
a starving writer who
drinks.
drunks are never forgiven
anything.

but when the world is closing in very
fast
a bottle of wine seems a very
reasonable friend.

ah. all those landladies,
most of them heavy, slow, their husbands
long dead, I can still see those
dears
climbing up and down the stairways of
their world.

they ruled my very existence:
without them allowing me
an extra week on the rent
now and then,
I was out on the
street

and I couldn't WRITE
on the street.
it was very important to have a
room, a door, those
walls.

oh, those dark mornings
in those beds
listening to their footsteps
listening to them cough

hearing the flushing of their
toilets, smelling the cooking of
their food
while waiting
for some word
on my submissions to New York City
and the world,
my submissions to those educated,
intelligent, snobbish, inbred,
formal, comfortable people
out there

they truly took their time to
say, no.

yes, in those dark beds
with the landladies rustling about
puttering and snooping, sharpening
utensils,
I often thought of those editors and
publishers out there
who didn't recognize
what I was trying to say
in my special
way

and I thought, they must be
wrong.

then this would be followed
with a thought much worse
than that:

I could be a
fool:

almost every writer thinks
they are doing
exceptional work.

that's
normal.

being a fool is
normal.

and then I'd
get out of bed
find a piece of
paper
and start
writing
again.

they don't eat like us

my father eating.

his ears moved.

he munched with great vigor.

I wished him in hell.

I watched the fork in his hand.
I watched it put food into his mouth.

the food I ate was tasteless and deadly.
his small bits of conversation entered my head.
the words ran down my spine.
they spilled into my shoes.

"eat your food, Henry," my mother said.

he said, "many people are starving and don't eat as well as us!"

I wished him in hell.
I watched his fork.
it gathered more food and put it into his mouth.
he chewed in a dog-like fashion.
his ears moved.

the brutal beatings he gave me I was ready for.
but watching him eat brought on the darkness.
there at the tablecloth.
there with the green and blue wooden napkin holders.

"eat your food or I'll strop your god damned ass," he told me.

later in life I made him pay somewhat.
but he still owes me.

and I'll never collect.

let me tell you

hell is built
piece by piece
brick by brick
around
you.
it's a gradual,
not a rapid
process.

we build our
own
inferno,
blame
others.

but hell is
hell.

wordly hell is
hell.

my hell and
your
hell.

our
hell.

hell, hell,
hell.

the song of
hell.

putting your
shoes on
in the
morning.
hell.

blasted apart with the first breath

running out of days
as the banister glints
in the early morning sun.

there will be no rest
even in our dreams.

now, all there is to do is
reset
broken moments.

when even to exist seems a
victory
then surely our luck has
run thin

thinner than a bloody stream
toward death.

life is a sad song:
we have heard too many
voices
seen too many
faces
too many
bodies

worst have been the faces:
a dirty joke that no one
can understand.

barbaric, senseless days total
in your skull;
reality is a juiceless
orange.

there is no plan
no out
no divinity
no sparrow of
joy.

we can't compare life to
anything—that's
too dreary a
prospect.

relatively speaking,
we were never short on
courage

but, at best, the odds
remained long
and
at worst,
unchangeable.

and what was worst:
not that we wasted
it
but that it was
wasted
on us:

coming out of
the Womb
trapped
in light and
darkness

stricken and numbed

alone in the temperate zone of
dumb agony

now

    running out of days
as the banister glints
in the early morning sun.

Elvis lives

the boy was going to take the bus out
to see the
Graceland Mansion

then
the Greyhound Lines went
on strike.

there were only two clerks
and two lines
at the station
and the lines were
50 to 65 people
long.

after two hours in line
one of the clerks told the
boy
that his bus
would leave
as soon as the substitute
driver arrived.

"when will that be?" the
boy asked.

"we can't
be certain," the
clerk answered.

the boy slept on the floor
that night
but by 9 a.m.
the next morning
the substitute driver
still had not
arrived.

the boy had to wait
in another line
to get to the
toilet.

he finally got a
stall, carefully
fitted the
sanitary toilet seat
paper cover,
pulled down his
pants,
his shorts
and
sat down.

luckily
the boy had a
pencil.

he found a clean
space
among all the
smeared and demented
scrawlings and
drawings

and very
carefully
and
heavily
he printed:

HEARTBREAK HOTEL

then he dropped the
first
one.

my buddy in valet parking at the racetrack:

after 9 long races among greedy faces
on a hot Sunday that hardly rhymes with
reason
I have murdered another day,
come out with shoelaces flopping (while
secretly craving to be in a moss-
lined cave, say,
watching black and white cartoons
while wanton simplicity soothes the
muddled brain)
as my buddy the valet races the
machine up, revving the 8-year-
old engine, he leaps
out:
"how ya doin', baby?"
"things have me by the jugular, Frank,
I'm ready to run up the white
flag."
"not *you*, baby, you're my
leader!"
"you can do better than that,
Frank . . ."

I get in, hook the seat belt, put on
the driving glasses, put it in first . . .

"hey, man," he sticks his head into the
window, "let's go out and get drunk and
kick some ass and find some
pussy!"

I tell him, "I'll consider that."

as I pull out I can see him in the rear-

view mirror: he's giving me the
finger.

I smile for the first time in 7 or
8 hours.

see here, you

blazing bastard fools
poets
with your
idiot scrolls
you are so
pompous
in your
knowledge
so
assured
that you are
on a hot roll
to
nirvana

you
soft lumps of
humanity

you
imitators of
other
pretenders

you are still
in
the shadow of
the
Mother

you
have never
bargained with
the
Beast

you have never
tasted
the full flavor of
Hell

you have never
seen
the Edge of
yourself

you have never
been alone
with the
razor-sharp
walls

you
blazing bastard fools
with your
idiot scrolls

there is nothing
to
know

no place
to
travel

your
lives
your
deaths
your
idiot
scrolls

useless

disgusting

and

not as real
as

the
wart
on the ass
of
a
hog.

you
are rejected by
circumstance.

good
bye.

spark

I always resented all the years, the hours, the
minutes I gave them as a working stiff, it
actually hurt my head, my insides, it made me
dizzy and a bit crazy—I couldn't understand the
murdering of my years
yet my fellow workers gave no signs of
agony, many of them even seemed satisfied, and
seeing them that way drove me almost as crazy as
the dull and senseless work.

the workers submitted.
the work pounded them to nothingness, they were
scooped-out and thrown away.

I resented each minute, every minute as it was
mutilated
and nothing relieved the monotony.

I considered suicide.
I drank away my few leisure hours.

I worked for decades.

I lived with the worst kind of women, they killed what
the job failed to kill.

I knew that I was dying.
something in me said, go ahead, die, sleep, become as
them, accept.

then something else in me said, no, save the tiniest
bit.
it needn't be much, just a spark.
a spark can set a whole forest on
fire.
just a spark.
save it.

I think I did.
I'm glad I did.
what a lucky god damned
thing.

the science of physiognomy

long gone along the way, faces
grey and white and black and brown, and
eyes, all color of eyes.
eyes are odd, I have lived with a woman,
at least one, where the sex was fair, the
conversation passable and sometimes there was
even a seeming love
but then I suddenly noticed the eyes, saw there
the dark smeared walls of a stinking
hell.

(of course, I am pleased that I do not often have to
see my own eyes, lips, hair, ears, so
forth—
I avoid the mirror with a studied
regularity.)

long gone along the way, he had a face like a
mole pie, fat and unshivering and he walked up to
me in the railroad yards, I was beastly sick
and that flesh plate shook my innards, my psycho-
kid insides as he said, "I'm waiting on my pay-
check, I been squeezing this nickel so hard that the
buffalo is screaming." he showed me the
nickel.
tough, but no beer, I walked away from him,
my face white like a bright headlight, I walked
away from him and toward the faces of the non-
whites who
hated me with a natural
ease.

long gone along the way, the landladies' faces,
doomed, powdered, old lilac faces, old lovely dolls
with husbands so long gone, the agony diminished but
still there as I followed them up stairways nearly a
century old to some cubicle of a room and I always

told them, "ah, a very nice room . . ."; to pay
then, close the door, undress, lay upon that
bed and turn out the light (it was always early
evening) and then soon to hear the same sound:
the scurry of my old friends: either the roaches or
the mice or the rats.

long gone along the way, now I wonder about Inez
and Irene and their sky-blue eyes and their wonderful
legs and breasts
but mostly
their faces, faces carved out of a marble that
sometimes the gods
bestow and
Inez and Irene sat in front of me in class and learned about
algebra, the shortest distance between two points, the
Treaty of Versailles, about Attila the Hun and
etc.
and I watched them and *wondered* what they were
thinking?
nothing much,
probably.
and I wonder where they are tonight
with their faces these 5 decades and 2 years
later?
the skin which covers the bone, the eyes that
smile; quick, turn out the light, let the dark
dance . . .

the most beautiful face I ever saw was that of a
paperman, a newsboy, the old fellow so long gone
down the way
who sat at a stand at Beverly and Vermont,
his head, his face looked like what they
called him: The Frog Man. I saw him
often but we seldom spoke and
The Frog Man died suddenly
and was gone
but I will always remember him
and one night

I came out of a nearby bar,
he was there at his stand and
he looked at me and said, "you and I, we know the same
things."

I nodded, put both thumbs up, and that big Frog
face, the big Frog head lifted in the moonlight
and began laughing the most terrible and real
laughter I have ever
heard.

long gone along the way

victory

what bargains we have made
we have
kept
and
as the dogs of the hours
close in
nothing
can be taken
from us
but
our lives.

Edward Sbragia

puffing on tiny cigarette butts as the world washes to the
shore I
burn my
dumb lips
think of
Manfred Freiherr von Richthofen
und sein
Fliegerzirkus.

as my cat sits in the bathroom window I
light a new
stub

as Norway winks and the dogs of hell pray for
me

downstairs my wife studies the
Italian
language.

up here
I would give half my ass for a
decent
smoke . . .

I
sneeze
then
jump: a little red coal of ash has dropped onto my
white white
belly—I
dig the fiery bit out with my
fingers:
a bit of minor
pain

I type naked: see my sulking soul
now
with a little pink
dot.

you see, I have my own show going on up
here, I don't need Vegas or cable
tv,
the label on my wine bottle states
in part:

"... *our winemaker, Edward Sbragia, has retained the
fresh, fruity character of the Pinot Noir and Napa
Gamay grapes* ..."

the dogs of hell pray for me as the
world washes to the
shore.

wandering in the cage

languid conjecture during hours of moil, trapped in the shadows
of the father.
sidewalks outside of cafes are lonely
through the day.

my cat looks at me and is not sure what I am and
I look back and am pleased to feel
the same
about him . . .

reading 2 issues of a famous magazine of 40 years
ago, the writing that I felt was bad then,
I still feel
is
that way

and none of the writers have lasted.

sometimes there is a strange justice
working
somewhere.

sometimes
not . . .

grammar school was the first awakening of a long hell
to come:
meeting other beings as horrible as my
parents.

something I never thought
possible . . .

when I won the medal for Manual of Arms in the
R.O.T.C.
I wasn't interested in
winning.

I wasn't much interested in anything, even the
girls seemed a bad game
to chase: all too much for all too
little

at night before sleeping I often considered what I
would do, what I would be:
bank robber, drunk, beggar, idiot, common
laborer.

I settled on idiot and common laborer, it
seemed more comfortable than any of the
alternatives . . .

the best thing about near-starvation and hunger is
that when you finally
eat
it is such a beautiful and delicious and
magical thing.

people who eat 3 meals a day throughout life
have never really
tasted
food . . .

people are strange: they are constantly angered by
trivial things,
but on a major matter
like
totally wasting their lives,
they hardly seem to
notice . . .

on writers: I found out that most of them
swam together.
there were schools, establishments,
theories.
groups gathered and fought each
other.
there was literary politics.

there was game-playing and
bitterness.

I always thought writing was a
solitary profession.

still do . . .

animals never worry about
Heaven or Hell.

neither do
I.

maybe that's why
we
get along . . .

when lonely people come around
I soon can understand why
other people leave them
alone.

and that which would be a
blessing to
me

is a horror to
them . . .

poor poor Celine.
he only wrote one book.
forget the others.
but what a book it was:
Voyage au bout de la nuit.
it took everything out of
him.
it left him a hopscotch
odd-ball
skittering through the

fog of
eventuality . . .

the United States is a very strange
place: it reached its apex in
1970
and since then
for every year
it has regressed
3 years,
until now
in 1989
it is 1930
in the way of
doing things.

you don't have to go to the movies
to see a horror
show.

there is a madhouse near the post office
where I mail my works
out.

I never park in front of the post office,
I park in front of the madhouse
and walk down.

I walk past the madhouse.

some of the lesser mad are allowed
out on the porch.
they sit like
pigeons.

I feel a brotherhood with
them.
but I don't sit with them.

I walk down and drop my works
in the first class slot.

I am supposed to know what I am
doing.

I walk back, look at them and
don't look at
them.

I get in my car and drive
off.

I am allowed to drive a
car.

I drive it all the way back to my
house.

I drive my car up the driveway,
thinking,
what am I doing?

I get out of my car
and one of my 5 cats walks up to
me, he is a very fine
fellow.

I reach down and touch
him.

then I feel all right.

I am exactly what I am supposed to
be.

the pack

the dogs are at it again; they leap and
tear, back off, circle, then
attack again.

and I had thought this was over, I had
thought that they had
forgotten; now there are only
more of them.

and I am older,
now

but the dogs are
ageless

and as always they tear not only at
the flesh but also at
the mind and the spirit.

now
they are circling me
in this room.

they are not
beautiful; they are the dogs
from hell

and they will find you
too

even though you are one
of them
now.

question and answer

he sat naked and drunk in a room of summer
night, running the blade of the knife
under his fingernails, smiling, thinking
of all the letters he had received
telling him that
the way he lived and wrote about
that—
it had kept them going when
all seemed
truly
hopeless.

putting the blade on the table, he
flicked it with a finger
and it whirled
in a flashing circle
under the light.

who the hell is going to save
me? he
thought.

as the knife stopped spinning
the answer came:
you're going to have to
save yourself.

still smiling,
a: he lit a
cigarette
b: he poured
another
drink
c: gave the blade
another
spin.

fan letter

I been readin' you for a long time now,
I just put Billy Boy to bed,
he got 7 mean ticks from somewhere,
I got 2,
my husband, Benny, he got 3.
some of us love bugs, others hate
them.
Benny writes poems.
he was in the same magazine as you
once.
Benny is the world's greatest writer
but he got this temper.
he gave a readin' once and somebody
laughed at one of his serious poems
and Benny took his thing out right
there
and pissed on stage.
he says you write good but that you
couldn't carry his balls in a paper
bag.
anyhow, I made a BIG POT OF MARMALADE
tonight,
we all just LOVE marmalade here.
Benny lost his job yesterday, he told his
boss to stick it up his ass
but I still got my job down at the
manicure shop.
you know fags come in to get their nails
done?
you aren't a fag, are you, Mr.
Chinaski?
anyhow, I just felt like writing you.
your books are read and read around
here.
Benny says you're an old fart, you
write pretty good but that you
couldn't carry his balls in a

paper sack.
do you like bugs, Mr. Chinaski?
I think the marmalade is cool enough to
eat now.
so goodbye.

Dora

hold on, it's a belly laugh

it would be good to get
out of here,
just go,
pop off, get away from
memories of this
and all
that,
but staying has its
flavor too:
all those babes who
thought they were
hot numbers
now living in dirty
flats
while looking forward
to the next
episode on
some Soap Opera,
and all those guys,
those who really
thought
they were going to
make it,
grinning in the
Year Book with their
tight-skinned
mugs,
now they are
cops,
clerk typists,
operators of
sandwich stands,
horse grooms,
plops
in the dust.

it's good to stay
around
to see what
happened to
all the
others—only
when you go to
the bathroom,
avoid the
mirror
and
don't look
at
what you
flush
away.

finished

the ball comes up to the
plate and I can't
see
it.

my batting average has dropped to
.231

small things constantly
irritate me
and I can't sleep
nights.

"you'll come back,
Harry," my teammates
tell me.

then they grin and are
secretly
pleased.

I've been benched for a
22 year old
kid.

he looks good up there:
power, lots of line
drives.

"ever thought of coaching?"
the manager asks.

"no," I tell him, "how about
you?"

when I get home my wife
asks, "you get in the line-
up tonight?"

"nope."

"don't worry, he'll put you
in."

"no, he won't. I'm gonna
pinch hit the rest of the
season."

I go into the bathroom and
look into the
mirror.

I'm no 22 year old
kid.

what gets me is that it
seemed to happen
overnight.

one night I was good.
the next night, it
seemed, I was
finished.

I come out of the bathroom
and my wife says,
"don't worry, all you need
is a little
rest."

"I been thinking about going
into coaching," I tell
her.

"sure," she says, "and after
that I'll bet you'll be a
good manager."

"hell yes," I say, "anything
on tv?"

zero

dark taste in mouth, my neck is stiff, I am looking for
my sonic vibrator, the music on my radio is diseased,
the winds of death seep through my slippers, and a
terrible letter in the mail today from a pale non-
soul
who requests that he may come by to see me
in repayment, he says, for a ride he gave me home
from a drunken Pasadena party
20 years ago.
also, one of the cats shit on the rug this
morning
and in the first race I bet this afternoon
the horse tossed the jock
coming out of the gate.

downstairs
I have a large photo of Hemingway
drunk before noon in Havana, he's on the floor
mouth open, his big belly trying to flop
out of his shirt.

I feel like that photo and I'm not even drunk.
maybe
that's the problem.

whatever the problem is, it's there, and worse, it
shouldn't be
for I have been a lucky man, I shouldn't even
be here
after all I have done to myself
and after all they have done
to me
I ought to be kneeling to the gods and giving
thanks.
instead, I deride their kindness by being
impatient
with the world.

maybe a damned good night's sleep will bring me back
to a gentle sanity.
but at the moment, I look about this room and, like
myself, it's all in disarray: things fallen
out of place, cluttered, jumbled, lost, knocked
over, and I can't put it straight, don't
want to.

perhaps living through these petty days will get us ready
for the dangerous ones.

eyeless through space

it's no longer any good, sucker, they've
turned out the lights, they've
blocked the rear entrance
and
the front's on fire;
nobody knows your name;
down at the opera they play
checkers;
the city fountains piss
blood;
the extremities are reamed
and
they've hung the best
barber;
the dim souls have ascended;
the cardboard souls smile;
the love of dung is unanimous;
it's no longer any good, sucker, the
graves have emptied out onto the
living;
last is first,
lost is everything;
the giant dogs mourn through dandelion
dreams;
the panthers welcome cages;
the onion heart is frosted,
destiny is destitute,
the horns of reason are muted as
the laughter of fools blockades the air;
the champions are dead
and
the newly born are smitten;
the jetliners vomit the eyeless through
space;
it's no longer any good, sucker, it's been
getting to that
right along

and now
it's here
and you can't touch it smell it see it
because it's nothing everywhere as
you look up or down or turn or sit or stand
or sleep or run,
it's no longer any good, sucker.
it's no longer any good
sucker sucker sucker
and
if you don't already know
I'm not surprised
and
if you do, sucker, good
luck
in the dark
going nowhere.

tag up and hold

not much chance in
Amsterdam;
cheese dislikes the
flea;
the center fielder
turns
runs back
in his stupid
uniform,
times it all
perfectly:
ball and man
arriving as
one
he
gloves it
precisely
in tune with the
universe;
not much chance in
east
Kansas City;
and
have you noticed
how
men stand
side by side
in urinals,
trained in the
act,
looking straight
ahead;
the center fielder
wings it
into the
cut-off
man

who eyes the
runners;
the sun plunges
down
as somewhere
an old
woman
opens a window
looks at a
geranium,
goes for a cup of
water;
not much chance in
New York City

or
in the look
of the eye
of
the man
who sits in a
chair
across from
you

he is
going
to ask you
certain
questions about
certain
things

especially
about

what to
do

without
much chance.

upon this time

fine then, thunderclaps at midnight, death in the
plaza.
my shoes need shining.
my typewriter is silent.

I write this in pen
in an old yellow
notebook
while
leaning propped up against the wall
behind the
bed.

Hemingway said, "it won't come
anymore."
later—the gun
into the
mouth.

not writing is not good
but trying to write
when you can't is
worse.

hey, I have excuses:
I have TB and the
antibiotics dull the
brain.

"you'll write again," people
assure me, "you'll be
better than
ever."

that's nice to know.

but the typewriter is silent
and it looks at
me.

meanwhile, every two or three
weeks
I get a fan letter in the mail
telling me that
surely
I must be
the world's greatest
writer.

but
the typewriter is silent
and looks at
me. . . .

this is one of the
strangest times
of my
life.

I've got to do a
Lazarus
and I can't even
shine
my shoes.

Downtown Billy

they used to call him
"Downtown" Billy.

"Downtown" had these
long arms
and he swung them
with
abandon
and with great
force.

when you fought
"Downtown" Billy
you never knew
where the punches
were coming
from: "They come
from Downtown . . ."

"Downtown" once rose
all the way
to #4 in his weight
class,
then he dropped out
of the first
ten.

then he fell to
fighting 6 rounders,
then 4.

the punches still
came from
Downtown
but you could
see them
coming.

then he was just a
sparring
partner.

last I heard
he left
town.

today I feel
like "Downtown" Billy,
sitting in this
blue garden chair
under the
walnut
tree,
watching the
neighbor boy
bounce a
basketball,
take some
fancy steps
forward,
then loop the
ball
through the
hoop
over the
garage
door.

I have just taken
my
pills.

8 count

from my bed
I watch
3 birds
on a telephone
wire.

one flies
off.
then
another.

one is left,
then
it too
is gone.

my typewriter is
tombstone
still.

and I am
reduced to bird
watching.

just thought I'd
let you
know,
fucker.

ill

being very ill and very weak is a very strange
thing.
when it takes all your strength to get from the
bedroom to the bathroom and back, it seems like
a joke but
you don't laugh.

back in bed you consider death again and find
the same thing: the closer you get to it
the less forbidding it
becomes.

you have much time to examine the walls
and outside
birds on a telephone wire take on much
importance.
and there's the tv: men playing baseball
day after day.

no appetite.
food tastes like cardboard, it makes you
ill, more than
ill.

the good wife keeps insisting that you
eat.
"the doctor said . . ."

poor dear.

and the cats.
the cats jump up on the bed and look at me.
they stare, then jump
off.

what a world, you think: eat, work, fuck,
die.

luckily I have a contagious disease: no
visitors.

the scale reads 155, down from
217.

I look like a man in a death camp.
I
am.

still, I'm lucky: I feast on solitude, I
will never miss the crowd.

I could read the great books but the great books don't
interest me.

I sit in bed and wait for the whole thing to go
one way or the
other.

just like everybody
else.

only one Cervantes

it's no use, I've got to admit,
I am into my first real
writer's block
after over
5 decades
of typing.
I have some excuses:
I've had a long
illness
and I'm nearing the age of
70.
and when you're near
70 you always consider the
possibility of
slippage.
but I am bucked-up
by the fact that
Cervantes
wrote his greatest work
at the age of
80.
but how many
Cervantes
are there?

I've been spoiled with the
easy way I have created
things,
and now there's this
miserable
stoppage.

and now
spiritually constipated I've
grown testy,
have screamed at my wife
twice this week,

once smashing a glass
into the sink.
bad form,
sick nerves,
bad
style.

I should accept this
writer's block.
hell, I'm lucky I'm alive,
I'm lucky I don't have
cancer.
I'm lucky in a hundred
different ways.
sometimes at night
in bed
at one or two a.m.
I will think about
how lucky I am
and it keeps me
awake.

now I've always written in a
selfish way, that is, to please
myself.
by writing things down I have
been better able to
live with them.

now, that's
stopped.

I see other old men with canes
sitting at bus stop benches,
staring straight into the sun and
seeing nothing.
and I know there are other
old men
in hospitals and nursing
homes

sitting upright in their
beds
grunting over
bedpans.
death is nothing, brother,
it's life that's
hard.

writing has been my fountain
of youth,
my whore,
my love,
my gamble.

the gods have spoiled me.

yet look, I am still
lucky,
for writing about a
writer's block
is better than not writing
at all.

that I have known the dead

that I have known the dead and now I'm
dying
as they spoon succotash and
noodles
into a skull
past
caring.

that I have known the dead and now I'm
dying
in a world long ago
gone

leaving this is
nothing.
loving it was
too.

that I have known the dead and now I'm
dying
fingers thin to the
bone,
I offer no
prayers.

that I have known the dead and now I'm
dying

dying
I have known the dead

here on earth
and elsewhere;
alone now,
alone then,
alone.

are you drinking?

washed-up, on shore, the old yellow notebook
out again
I write from the bed
as I did last
year.

will see the doctor,
Monday.

"yes, doctor, weak legs, vertigo, head-
aches and my back
hurts."

"are you drinking?" he will ask.
"are you getting your
exercise, your
vitamins?"

I think that I am just ill
with life, the same stale yet
fluctuating
factors.

even at the track
I watch the horses run by
and it seems
meaningless.

I leave early after buying tickets on the
remaining races.

"taking off?" asks the mutuel
clerk.

"yes, it's boring,"
I tell him.

"if you think it's boring
out there," he tells me, "you oughta be
back here."

so here I am
propped against my pillows
again

just an old guy
just an old writer
with a yellow
notebook.

something is
walking across the
floor
toward
me.

oh, it's just
my cat

this
time.

"D"

the doctor is into collecting art
and the magazines in his waiting room
are Artsy
have thick covers, glistening pages,
and large color
photos.

the receptionist calls my name and
I'm led into a waiting room with
walls adorned with paintings
and a chart of the human
body.

the doctor enters: "how are you
doing?"

not well, I think, or I wouldn't
be here.

"now," he goes on, "I am surprised
by the biopsy, I didn't expect
this . . ."

the doctor is a bald, well-scrubbed
pink fellow.

"I can almost always tell just by
looking; this time, I
missed . . ."

he paused.

"go on," I say.

"all right, let's say there are
4 types of cancer—A, B, C, D.

well, you've got
D.
and if I had cancer I'd rather
have your kind:
D."

the doctor is in a tough business
but the pay is
good.

"well," he says, "we'll just burn it off,
o.k.?"

I stretch out on the table and he has an
instrument, I can feel the heat of it
searing through the air
but also
I hear a whirring sound
like a drill.

"it'll be over in a
blink . . ."

the small growth is just inside of
the right nostril.
the instrument touches it
and
the room is filled with the smell
of burning flesh.

then he stops.

then he starts
again.

there is pain but it's sharp and
centered.

he stops
again.

"now we are going to do it
once more to
clean it
up."

he applies the instrument
again.
this time I feel the most
pain.

"there now . . ."

it's finished, no bandage needed,
it's
cauterized.

then I'm at the receptionist's
desk, she makes out a bill, I
pay with my
Mastercard, am out the door,
down the stairway and there
in the parking lot
awaits
my faithful automobile.

It's a day with a great deal of
afternoon left

I light a cigarette, start the
car and
get the hell
out of there
moving toward something
else.

in the bottom

in the bottom of the hour
lurks
the smoking claw
the red train
the letter home
the deep-fried blues.

in the bottom of the hour
lurks
the song you sang together
the mouse in the attic
the train window in the rain
the whiskey breath on grandfather
the coolness of the jail trustee.

in the bottom of the hour
lurks
the famous gone quite stupid
churches with peeling white paint
lovers who chose hyenas
schoolgirls giggling at atrophy
the suicide oceans of night.

in the bottom of the hour
lurks
button eyes in a cardboard face
dead library books squeezed upright.

in the bottom of the hour
lurks
the octopus
Gloria gone mad while shaving her armpits
the gang wars
no toilet paper at all in a train station restroom
a flat tire halfway to Vegas.

in the bottom of the hour
lurks
the dream of the barmaid as the perfect girl
the first and only home run
the father sitting in the bathroom with the door open
the brave and quick death
the gang rape in the Fun House.

in the bottom of the hour
lurks
the wasp in the spider web
the plumbers moving to Malibu
the death of the mother like a bell that never rang
the absence of wise old men.

in the bottom of the hour
lurks
Mozart
fast food joints where the price of a bad meal exceeds the hourly wage
angry women and deluded men and faded children
the housecat
love as a swordfish.

in the bottom of the hour
lurks
17,000 people screaming at a homerun
millions laughing at the obvious jokes of a tv comedian
the long and hideous wait in the welfare offices
Cleopatra fat and insane
Beethoven in the grave.

in the bottom of the hour
lurks
the damnation of Faust and sexual intercourse
the sad-eyed dogs of summer lost in the streets
the last funeral
Celine failing again
the carnation in the buttonhole of the kindly killer.

in the bottom of the hour
lurks
fantasies tainted with milk
our obnoxious invasion of the planets
Chatterton drinking rat poison
the bull that should have killed Hemingway
Paris like a pimple in the sky.

in the bottom of the hour
lurks
the mad writer in a cork room
the falseness of the Senior Prom
the submarine with purple footprints.

in the bottom of the hour
lurks
the tree that cries in the night
the place that nobody found
being so young you thought you could change it
being middle-aged and thinking you could survive it
being old and thinking you could hide from it.

in the bottom of the hour
lurks
2:30 a.m.
and the next to last line
and then the last.

the creative act

for the broken egg on the floor
for the 5th of July
for the fish in the tank
for the old man in room 9
for the cat on the fence

for yourself

not for fame
not for money

you've got to keep chopping

as you get older
the glamour recedes

it's easier when you're young

anybody can rise to the
heights now and then

the buzzword is
consistency

anything that keeps it
going

this life dancing in front of
Mrs. Death.

a suborder of naked buds

the uselessness of the word is
evident.
I would like to make
this
piece of paper
shriek and dance and
laugh
but
the keys just
strike it harmlessly
and
we settle
for just a fraction of
the whole.

this incompleteness is all
we have:
we write the same things
over and over
again.
we are fools,
driven.

the uselessness of the word is
evident.

writers can only pretend to
succeed
some pretend well, others
not so

yet
none of us come
near
none of us even
close

sitting at these
machines

behooved to
live
out
our indecent
profession.

companion

I am not alone.
he's here now.
sometimes I think he's
gone
then he
flies back
in the morning or at
noon or in the
night.
a bird no one wants.
he's mine.
my bird of pain.
he doesn't sing.
that bird
swaying on the
bough.

you know and I know and thee know

that as the yellow shade rips
as the cat leaps wild-eyed
as the old bartender leans on the wood
as the hummingbird sleeps

you know and I know and thee know

as the tanks practice on false battlefields
as your tires work the freeway
as the midget drunk on cheap bourbon cries alone at night
as the bulls are carefully bred for the matadors
as the grass watches you and the trees watch you
as the sea holds creatures vast and true

you know and I know and thee know

the sadness and the glory of two slippers under a bed
the ballet of your heart dancing with your blood
young girls of love who will someday hate their mirrors
overtime in hell
lunch with sick salad

you know and I know and thee know

the end as we know it now
it seems such a lousy trick after the lousy agony but

you know and I know and thee know

the joy that sometimes comes along out of nowhere
rising like a falcon moon across the impossibility

you know and I know and thee know

the cross-eyed craziness of total elation
we know that we finally have not been cheated

you know and I know and thee know

as we look at our hands our feet our lives our way
the sleeping hummingbird
the murdered dead of armies
the sun that eats you as you face it

you know and I know and thee know

we will defeat death.

3

the sun slants in
like a golden sword
as the odds grow
shorter

show biz

I can't have it
and you can't have it
and we won't
get it

so don't bet on it
or even think about
it

just get out of bed
each morning

wash
shave
clothe
yourself
and go out into
it

because
outside of that
all that's left is
suicide and
madness

so you just
can't
expect too much

you can't even
expect

so what you do
is
work from a modest
minimal
base

like when you
walk outside
be glad your car
might possibly
be there

and if it is—
that the tires
aren't
flat

then you get
in
and if it
starts—you
start.

and
it's the damndest
movie
you've ever
seen
because
you're
in it—

low budget
and
4 billion
critics

and the longest
run
you ever hope
for
is

one
day.

darkness & ice

I am spooked by the bluebells and the silent harp while
passing down Western Avenue and seeing the tombstones
placed flat instead of upright upon the cemetery lawn: our decent
modernity not wanting to upset us with Finalities while we
pay 22% interest on our credit cards.

I follow the street on down
feeling wonderful that I do not appear to be lost.
we need our landmarks (like cemeteries), we need our
liquor and our liabilities.
we need so many things we think we do not
need.

strangely then, as I drive south, I begin thinking about
THE WORLD IS SQUARE, INC., an institution which meets and
discusses the fact that: the world is square and the North Pole is at
the CENTER of the SQUARE and holds everything from sliding
over the edge and that the EDGE is really a WALL OF
DARKNESS AND ICE and that nothing or nobody can go *through*
and that
when we THINK we are circling the globe we are only
CIRCLING the SQUARE, finally arriving back
where we began.

I wait at a signal, the light turns green and I move on
thinking, well, maybe the planets we believe are round are
illusions, and the moon and the sun, they are really square
too.

well, you can't rule anything out; I vote for round
but I still realize that it wasn't too long ago when
EVERYBODY thought the answer was SQUARE.

I stop at another signal, wait, while being held from falling
over the EDGE OF DARKNESS AND ICE by the North Pole
        standing in the
CENTER of the SQUARE.

the light changes, I drive on, turn left, go a few blocks, turn
right, go a block or so, turn left, go a block, turn right, then
a left and I am at my driveway, turn in, drive slowly up to
the garage
past the tangerine tree and the tangerines are round but
the garage door is square and I am still spooked by the
bluebells and the silent harp
cut the engine
get out
stand up
still alive.

I move along the walk.
god, things are getting interesting again: they say there are
bottomless craters at the North Pole and deep in the earth live
Creatures from Outer Space
down there
in a marvelous, beautiful and peaceful Kingdom, I move toward the
door, make ready to open it, not at all sure of what will be
waiting on the other side—there is always this gnarling
apprehension
generally but not always warranted, and as the North Pole holds me
from falling off either the Curve or the
Edge
I push open the wooden wall and enter, ready and not ready
enough.

the big ride

all right,
some day you'll see me in a plastic
helmet, long stockings,
double-lens goggles;
I'll be tooling along on my 10-
speed bike on the promenade,
my face will be as intense
as a canteloupe and
in my knapsack
there could be a
bible, along with the
liverwurst sandwich and
the red red
apple.

off to one side the
sea will break and
break
and I will
pump along—a
well-lived
man,
lived a little, per-
haps, beyond his
sensibilities: too
much hair in the
ears, and face
badly shaven;
there, my lips
never again to
kiss a
virgin; I gulp in
the salty air
while being
unsure of the
time
but almost sure

of the
place.

all right, gliding
along
girding up for the
casket,
the sun like a
yellow glove to
grab me
I pass a group of
young ones
sitting in their
convertible.

"Jesus Christ," I hear
a voice, "do you
know who that
was?"

was?
was?

why, you little
fart bells!
you bits of
bunny
droppings!

I kick it
into high, I
rise over a
hill
into a patch
of fog,
my legs
pump and
the
sea
breaks.

small cafe

you take a stool, unfold the paper, the waitress brings the
java, you order bacon and
everybody in there is old and bent and poor, they are like
the oldest people in the universe
having breakfast
and it's dark in there like the inside of a glove
and some of the patrons speak to each other,
only their voices are broken and scratched and they speak
of simple things,
so simple
you think that they are joking but
they hulk over their food, unsmiling . . .
"Casmir died, he wore his green shoes . . ."
"yeh."

strange place there, no sadness, no rancor, an overhead
fan turns slowly, one of the blades bent a bit, it
clicks against the grate: "a-flick, a-flick, a-flick . . ."
nobody
notices.

my food arrives, it is hot and clean, but never coffee
like that (the worst), it is like drinking the water left in muddy
footprints.

the old waitress is a dear, dressed in faded pink, she can
hardly walk, she's
sans everything.

"do you really love me?" she asks the young Mexican fry
cook. "why?"

"because I can't help it," he says, running the spatula
under a mass of hash browns, turning
them.

I eat, peruse the newspaper, general idea I get is
that the world is not yet about to end but a
recession is to come creeping in wearing
faded tennis
shoes.

an old man looms in the doorway, he's big in all the
wrong ways and shuts out what little light there
is.

"hey, anybody seen Vern?"

there is no answer, the old man
waits, he waits a good minute and a half, then he lets out a
little fart.
I can hear it, everybody can.   uh
huh.
he reaches up, scratches behind his left ear, then backs out of
the doorway and is
gone.

"that ratfucker," somebody says, "zinched little Laura out of
her dowry."

the last bit of toast sogs down my throat, I wipe my mouth, leave
the tip, rise to pay the
bill.

the cash register is the old fashioned kind where the
drawer jumps out when you hit the
keys.

I was the last person to sit down to eat, I am the first to
leave, the others still sit
fiddling with their food, fighting the coffee
down

as I get to my car I start the engine, think,
nice place, rather like an accidental
love, maybe I'll go back there

once or
twice.

then I back out, swing around and enter the
real world
again.

washrag

leaving for the track in the morning
my wife asks me,
"did you wring out your washrag
properly?"

"yes," I say.

"you never do," she says,
"it's important that you wring out
your washrag
properly."

I get into my car,
start it,
back out the drive.

of course, she's right, it is
important.
on the other hand
I don't want to get into an
argument over
washrags.

she waves goodbye,
I wave back,
then I turn left,
go down the hill.

it is a fine sunny
day
and great matters loom
across the horizon
of
history.
Carthage in my rearview
mirror,
I blend into
Time.

sitting with the IBM

another still, hot summer night,
the small insects circle my wineglass, my
winebottle.

I once again consider my death
as a Brahms symphony ends upon the
radio.

the horses didn't run today (not
here) but there was gunfire, murder,
bombings in many parts of the
earth.
there is always a contest
of sorts
at hand.

and the years move slow and the years
move fast and the years move
past.

it seems not so long ago that
old Henry Miller was still
alive,
always finding new young girls to dust
his lampshades, pose for him, and make him
nice little meals.
what a ladies' man, he could never get
enough of them.

anyhow, my 5 cats dislike the heat, they
sit outside under the cool juniper bushes
listening to me
type.
sometimes they bring me presents:
birds or mice.
then we have a little misunder-
standing.

and they back off
looking at me
and their eyes say: this guy's nuts,
he doesn't know that this is the way
it works.

another hot summer night as I sit here
and play at being a writer
again.
and the worst thing
of course
is that the words will never
truly break through for any of
us.

some nights I have taken the sheet
out of the typer and
held it over the cigarette
lighter, flicked
it and waited for the
result.

"Hank, are you burning things again?"
my wife will ask.

anyhow, there's another composer on the
radio now
and there is only so much he can do
with his notes.
I am proud for him and yet
sad for him too.

the radio is old and dusty
and through
the speaker
he talks to me.

it's as if he were hiding in there
and I want to console him, say:

"I am sorry, poor fellow, but
creation has its
limits."

another hot summer night
another sheet of paper in this machine,
more insects, more cigarettes in
this place, this time, hurrah hurrah, lost
in the grisly multitude of days
the speaker in the radio vibrates, trembles
as the composer swells out at me, the
son of a bitch is good
so brave despite his limitations
as the cats wait under the juniper
bushes and I pour more wine, more wine,
more wine.

my buddy, the buddha

I must wash this buddha that sits on my desk—
dust and grime all over him
mostly on his chest and belly; ah,
we have endured many long nights together; we have
endured trivia and horror; at unseemly times we
have laughed
cleanly—now
the least he deserves is a good
going over
with a wet rag;
truly terrible have been
some long nights but
the buddha has been good, quiet
company; he never quite looks at me but
he seems to be forever laughing—he's
laughing at this muck of
existence: there's nothing to be done.

"why clean me?" he now asks, "I will only dirty
again."
"I am only pretending at some dumb sanity," I
answer.
"drink your wine," he responds, "that's what
you're good at."
"and," I ask, "what are you good
at?"
he returns: "I am good at almost watching
you."

then he becomes silent.
he holds a circle of beads with a
tassel.

how did he get in
here?

the interviewers

the interviewers come around
and there is nothing that you can
really
tell them.

it's
embarrassing
and the easiest way out
is to get yourself
and them
drunk.

sometimes there is also a
camera man and a sound
man
and so it becomes a
party with
many bottles
needed.

I don't think they want to
hear the literary crap
either.

it seems to work out all
right:
I get letters
later:

"I really had a good
time . . ."

or: "it was the best time
I *ever* had."

how strange, when all I
remember

of any particular night is
saying goodbye at the
door
with: "don't leave
anything behind so you
have to
come back."

freaky time

the lady down at the end of the bar keeps looking at
me, I put my head down, I look away, I light
a cigarette, glance again: she's still staring at me, she's
charmingly dressed and she, herself, well, you might
say she's beautiful.
her eyes meld with mine; I am
elated and nervous, then
she gets up, goes to the ladies' room:
such a behind!
such grace!
what a gazelle!

I glance at my face in the bar mirror, look
away.

she's back; then the barkeep comes down: "a drink
from the lady at the end of the bar."

I nod thanks to her, lift my drink, smile, have a
hit.

she is looking again, what a strange and pleasur-
able experience.

I look forward, examine the backs of my hands—not
bad hands as far as hands go.

then, at once, it occurs to me:
she has mistaken me for somebody
else.

I leave my stool and slowly walk to the exit,
and out into the night; I walk half a block down the
boulevard, feel the need for a smoke, slip the
pack of cigarettes out of my coat pocket, look
curiously at the brand name (I did *not* purchase

these): DEATH, it
says.

I curse, hurl the pack into the street, move toward
the next bar: knew it all along: she was a
whore.

the aliens

you may not believe it
but there are people
who go through life with
very little
friction or
distress.
they dress well, eat
well, sleep well.
they are contented with
their family
life.
they have moments of
grief
but all in all
they are undisturbed
and often feel
very good.
and when they die
it is an easy
death, usually in their
sleep.

you may not believe
it
but such people do
exist.

but I am not one of
them.
oh no, I am not one
of them,
I am not even near
to being
one of
them

but they are
there

and I am
here.

shock treatment

the fight I saw,
after the tv cameras were
shut off,
a fighter in green
trunks and
a fighter in blue,
only 50 to 75
absolutely silent
people
remaining,
you heard each
blow
land
crushingly
amid
sweat, saliva
blood,
gasps of
agony,
drinks no longer
served,
all the lights
on,
thousands of
empty
seats,
the bell rang
to end the
round,
it clanged
right through
you
as the boxers
went back
sat on their
stools
and were

swabbed by
listless
cornermen.
we were all
in hell
all of us
and I
got up
and left
that time.

between races

I know that I'm not supposed to bother
you, he said.

you've got that right, I
answered.

but, he went on, I want to tell you
that I was up all night
reading your
latest book.
I've read all your
books.
I work in the
post office.

oh, I said.

and I want to interview you for
our newspaper.

no, I said, no
interview.

why? he asked.

I'm tired of interviews, they have
nothing to do with
anything.

listen, he went on, I'll make it
easy for you, I'll come to your
house or I'll buy you dinner at
Musso's.

no, thank you, I said.

look, the interview isn't really for
our paper, it's for
me, I'm a writer and I want to get
out of the post
office.

listen, I said, just pull up a chair
and sit down at your
typewriter.

no interview? he asked.

no, I answered.

he walked
off.

they were coming out on the track
for the next race.

talking to the young man had
made me feel
bad.

they thought that writing had
something to do with
the politics of the
thing.

they were simply not
crazy enough
in the head
to sit down to a
typer
and let the words bang
out.

they didn't want to
write

they wanted to
succeed at
writing.

I got up to make
my bet.

no use letting a little
conversation
ruin your
day.

splashing

dumb,
Jesus Christ,
some people are so dumb
you can hear them
splashing around
in their dumbness
as their eyes
look out of their
heads.
they have
most of their
parts: hands, feet,
ears, legs, elbows,
intestines, fingernails,
noses and so
forth
but
there's nothing
there
yet
they are able to
speak,
form sentences—
but what
comes out
of their mouths
are the stalest
concepts, the most
warped beliefs,
they are the repository
of all the obvious
stupidities
they have
stuffed
themselves
with

and it hurts me
to
look at them
to
listen to them,
I want to
run and hide
I want to
escape their engulfing
nullity

there is no
horror movie
worse,
no murder
as
unsolved

but
the world
goes on
and
they
go on

dumbly
slamming
my guts to
pieces.

darkling

some nights you don't sleep.
of course
having 3 or 4 cats on the bed
doesn't help.
my wife likes to carry them up
from downstairs
but
it's not always the cats, it's
hardly anything,
say,
re-working horse systems in my
brain, or it's a cold moon, an
itchy back, the
thought of death out
there
beyond the venetian blinds
or
I'll think nice things about my
wife, she looks so small there
under the blanket, a little
lump, that's all
(death, you take me first, please,
this lady needs a gentle space of
peace
without me).

then a boat horn blows from the
harbor.
I pull my head up, stretching
my thick neck, I see the
clock:
3:36 a.m.
that always does it: looking at
the clock.
by 3:45 a.m. I am asleep, just
like the cats, just like my

wife,
the venetian blinds closing us
all in.

Celine with cane and basket

tonight I am nothing
I have lost touch with the walls
I have seen too many heads, hands, feet,
heard too many voices,
I am weary with the continuation,
the music is old music,
there is no stirring in the air.

on my wall is a photo of
Celine,
he has a cane,
carries a basket,
wears a coat too heavy,
a long strand of hair falls across his face,
he has been stunned by life,
the dogs have had at him,
it got to be too much
much too much.

he walks through a small forest,
this doctor,
this typer of words,
all he wants to do is die,
that's all he wants,
and his photo is on the wall
and he is dead.

this year
1988
all these months
have had
a terribleness to them
that I have never felt
before.

I light a cigarette and
wait.

no more, no less

editor, critic, bigot, wit:
what do you expect of me
now that my youth has
flown and even my middle-
age is
gone?

I expect what I've always
expected:
the hard-driven line
and a bit of help
from the
gods.

as the walls get closer
there should be more to
say
instead of
less.

each day is still a
hammer,
a flower.

editor, critic, bigot, wit:
the grave has no
mirror

and I am still this
machine
this paper
and all the
etceteras.

the lost and the desperate

it was nice to be a boy in a dark movie house,
one entered the dream so much more easily
then.
I liked the French Foreign Legion movies
best and there were many of them
then.

I loved the forts and the sand and the
lost and desperate men.
these men were brave and they had beautiful
eyes.

I never saw men like that
in my neighborhood.
the neighborhood men were hunched and
miserable and angry and
cowardly.

I was going to join the French Foreign Legion.

I sat in the dark movie houses and I was
one of them.

we had been fighting for days without food
and with very little
water.

casualties had been horrendous.

our fort was surrounded, we were down to a
last few.
we propped up our dead comrades with
their rifles pointed toward the
desert
to make the Arabs think that they had not
killed many of us

otherwise we would have been
overwhelmed.

we ran from dead man to dead man
firing their rifles.
our sergeant was wounded
3 or 4 times but
he still commanded
screaming his orders.

then more of us died gallantly, then
we were down to the last two
(one of them the sergeant) but we
fought on, then we were out of
ammunition, the Arabs scaled the walls
on ladders and we knocked them back
with our rifle butts but more and more of
them were clambering over the walls, there
were too many
of them we were
finished, no chance, then there was the sound of a
BUGLE!
reinforcements were arriving!
fresh and rested upon the backs of thunderous
horses!
they charged en masse over the sand,
hundreds of them
dressed in bright and blazing uniforms.
the Arabs scattered down the walls
running for their horses and their
lives
but most of them were
doomed.

then the sergeant, knowing victory, was dying
in my arms.
"Chinaski," he said to me, "the fort is
ours!"
he gave a small smile, his head fell back and
he was gone.

then I was home again
I was back in my room.
a hunched, miserable and angry man
walked into the room and said,
"get out there now and mow the lawn.
I see a hair of grass sticking up!"

out there in the yard
I pushed the mower over the same grass
once more
back and forth
back and forth
wondering why all the brave men with
beautiful eyes were so far away,
wondering if they'd still be there
when I arrived.

the bully

actually, I do think that
my father was
insane,
the way he drove his
car,
honking,
cursing at people;
the way he got into
violent arguments
in public places
over the most
trivial incidents;
the way he beat
his only child
almost daily
upon the slightest
provocation.

of course, bullies
sometimes meet their
masters.

I remember once
entering the house
and my mother
told me,
"your father was
in a terrible
fight."

I looked for him,
found him sitting
on the toilet
with the bathroom
door
open.

his face was a mass of
bruises, welts,
puffed and black
eyes.
he even had a broken
arm
in a cast.

I was 13 years old.
I stood looking
at him.
I looked for
some time.

then he screamed,
"what the hell you
staring at!
what's your
problem?"

I looked at him
some more,
then walked
off.

it was to be
3 years later
that
I would knock him
on his
ass, no problem
with that
at
all.

downers

some people
grind away
making their
unhappiness
the ultimate
factor
of their
existence
until
finally
they are
just
automatically
unhappy,
their
suspicious
upset
snarling
selves
grinding

on
and
at
and
for
and
through

their only
relief
being

to meet
another
unhappy
person

or
to
create
one.

get close enough and you can't see

at this time
I know a couple of men
who seem to be in
love
while their ladies are treating
them
off-handedly or
worse.

these men are consumed by
their
ill-fate, can't
climb out of their
fix.

I too
have been in that
way,
only I was
worse
off:
I was charmed and
ensnared by
caseic beldames,
slimey slatterns,
inchoate prostitutes,
hypacodont
mesdames—
all the hustling
shrews of the
universe
found me,
and I
found them
wise
witty and

beautiful
then.

it was only after
some luck of
distance and time
that I was able to
realize
that
these ladies
were even less than
less.

so
now
when these men
tell me their sad
stories
there is nothing I can
say
because to me
their women look
like
hypacodont
beldames,
inchoate
slatterns,
caseic
mesdames
and
slimey
prostitutes,
not to mention
piss-biting
shrews

and they
most
probably
are.

true is true
enough,
yet
at small
tiny and
rare
moments

I wonder
what
I seemed
like
to my
ladies?

the beggars

the poor
in the grandstand section
playing the
daily doubles
the exactas
the pick-6's
the pick-9's

they have horrible
jobs
or
no jobs

they come in
beaten
to take another
beating.

scuffed shoes
shirts with buttons
missing,
faded and wrinkled
clothing—
muted eyes,
they are the
unwashed
the
unwanted

the beggars of the
grandstand

and as race after race
unfolds
they are routinely
sucked of
money and
hope

then
the last race is
over

and for a few
there's the
liquor
store

a bit to drink
and a
lottery
ticket.

for the
others:
nothing.

beggars of the
grandstand.

the State is going
to
make it.

the track is going
to
make
it

thanks to the
Days of the Living
Dead.

well,
the horses are
beautiful
anyhow.

the old horseplayer

he wears the same pants
the same coat
the same shoes
day after day.

his shirttail hangs out.
his shoes are unlaced.
his hair is white and
uncombed.
he is balding.

he walks slowly to make his
bets, then
walks slowly back to his
seat.

he watches each race
without emotion.

he is hooked on nothing but
an impossibility.

he is so tired.

the old horseplayer.

the skies, the mountains,
music, nothing matters to
him.

he's hooked on an
impossibility.

post time

some of the old rich still make it to
Santa Anita Turf Club parking.
and the old rich still buy Cadillacs—
and he can barely drive the Caddy—
and the valet helps them both
out.
he's fat and squat, very white, with
merry blue eyes and she's taller,
dignified but dumb, and her back is
bent.
expensively clothed
they both move toward the Turf Club
entrance
where they are swallowed forever
as the horn sounds to post
and the number one horse steps out
on the track
more beautiful than all the people
more beautiful than all the world
and it
begins.

off and on

at times I still consider coughing it up: gas pipe, 19th floor
window, 3 fifths of whiskey in 4 hours or
slamming at 85 mph into a slab of
concrete.

my first thought of suicide came at age 13 and it has
been with me ever since
through all the botched failures:
sometimes just rather playing at it, little minor
rehearsals;
other times
really trying like hell to
kill myself.

yet, now it's never totally intense, it's more like
considering whether to go to a movie or
not or whether to buy a new pair of
shoes.
actually, years go by and the suicidal thoughts
almost completely
abate.
then
suddenly
they return, like:
look here, baby, let's give it another
shot.

and when it returns it's fairly
compelling
but not so much in the mind (as in the old
days) but strangely, suicide waits in odd little places,
on the back of your neck or
at a spot just under the chin
or along the arms like the sleeves of a
sweater . . .
it used to hit the gut, now it's almost like

catching a
rash.

I will be driving along in my car with the radio
on and it will leap at me and I will smile at
it
remembering the old days
when those I knew thought that
my daring crazy acts stemmed from
bravery . . .

I will drive for several hours
up and down strange streets in
strange neighborhoods
at times
slowing down carefully
where children are playing in the
road.

I will park
go into cafes
drink coffee
read newspapers.
I will hear voices speaking of
ridiculous and dull
things.

I will be back in the car
driving along
and at once
everything will lift:
we all live in the same world:
I will have to pay my gas bill, get a
set of new reading glasses, I will need a
new tire
left rear
and I think I've been using my neighbor's
garbage can.

it is fine to be normal again and
as I pull into the driveway
a large white moon smiles at me
through the windshield of
evening.

I brake, get out, close the car
door, centuries of sadness, gladness and
equilibrium will walk with me up to the door
as I put in the key
unlock it
walk into the place
once again having escaped the
inescapable, I will move toward the
kitchen cabinet for the
bottle
to
celebrate
that
or
whatever there is,
isn't,
will be,
won't
be—
like right
now.

balloons

today they shot a guy who was
selling balloons at the
intersection.

they parked their cars at the
curbing
and called him
over.

he came
over.

they argued with him about
the price of a
balloon, they wanted him
to come down in
price.

he said he couldn't.

one of them started calling
him names.

the other took out a gun
and shot him in the
head.
twice.

he fell
right there
in the street.

they took his balloons,
said, "now we can
party," and then they
drove off

there are also other guys
at that intersection, they
sell oranges
mostly.

they left then
and they weren't at the
intersection the next day
or the next or
the next.

nobody was.

recognized

I was at the airport
standing at the arrival section
with my wife
waiting for her sister's
flight in
when a young man walked up:
"aren't you Henry Chinaski?"
"well, yes . . ."
"oh, I thought so!"
there was a pause.
then
he continued: "you don't
know what this
means to me!
I can't believe it!
I've read all your books!"
"thank you," I said, "I have to be
thankful for my
readers."
he gave me his name and we
shook hands.
"this is my wife," I started . . .
"*Sarah!*" he said, "I *know* her
from your books!"
another pause.
then:
"I get all your books from Red
down at Baroque . . .
I still can't believe it's
you!"
"it is," laughed my wife,
"it's him!"
"well," he said, "I'll leave you
alone now!"
"tell Red I said 'hello.' "
then the young man
moved off.

"he was all right," I said,
"I usually can't stand
them."

"like you say, you have to
be thankful for your
readers."

"damned right . . ."

then her sister's plane tooled
up and we moved with the others
to greet those we knew and those
who knew
us.

them and us

they were all out on the front porch
talking:
Hemingway, Faulkner, T. S. Eliot,
Ezra Pound, Hamsun, Wally Stevens,
e. e. cummings and a few others.

"listen," said my mother, "can't you
ask them to stop talking?"

"no," I said.

"they are talking garbage," said my
father, "they ought to get
jobs."

"they have jobs," I
said.

"like hell," said my
father.

"exactly," I
said.

just then Faulkner came
staggering in.
he found the whiskey in the
cupboard and went outside with
it.

"a terrible person,"
said my mother.

then she got up and peeked out
on the porch.

"they've got a woman with them,"
she said, "only she looks like a
man."

"that's Gertrude," I
said.

"there's another guy flexing his
muscles," she said, "he claims he
can whip any three of
them."

"that's Ernie," I said.

"and *he*," my father pointed to me,
"wants to be like *them!*"

"is that true?" my mother asked.

"not like them," I said, "but of
them."

"you get a god-damned job,"
said my father.

"shut up," I said.

"what?"

"I said, 'shut up,' I am listening to
these men."

my father looked at his wife:
"this is no son of
mine!"

"I hope not," I said.

Faulkner came staggering into the room
again.

"where's the telephone?" he
asked.

"what the hell for?" my father
asked.

"Ernie's just blown his brains
out," he said.

"you see what happens to men like
that?" screamed my father.

I got up
slowly
and helped Bill find
the
telephone.

luck was not a lady

being half-young I sat about the bars
in it up to the ears
thinking something might happen to
me, I mean, I tried the ladies:
"hey, baby, listen, the golden coast
weeps for your beauty . . ."
or some such.

their heads never turned, they looked
ahead, straight ahead,
bored.

"hey, baby, listen, I am a
genius, ha ha ha . . ."

silent before the bar mirror, these
magic creatures, these secret sirens,
big-legged, bursting out of their
dresses, wearing dagger
heels, earrings, strawberry mouths,
just sitting there, sitting there,
sitting there.

one of them told me, "you bore
me."

"no, baby, you got it
backwards . . ."

"oh, shut up."

then in would walk some dandy, some fellow
neat in a suit, pencil mustache, bow tie;
he would be slim, light, delicate
and so knowing
and the ladies would call his

name: "oh, Murray, Murray!"
or some such.

"hi, girls!"

I knew I could deck one of those
fuckers but that hardly mattered in the
scheme of things,
the ladies just gathered around Murray
(or some such) and I just kept ordering
drinks,
sharing the juke music with them
and listening to the laughter from
the outside.

I wondered what wonderful things
I was missing, the secret of the
magic, something that only they knew,
and I felt myself again the idiot in the
schoolyard, sometimes a man never got out
of there—he was marked, it could be told
at a glance

and so
I was shut out,
"I am the lost face of
Janus," I might say at some
momentary silence.
of course, to be
ignored.

they'd pile out
to cars parked in back
smoking
laughing
finally to drive off
to some consummate
victory

leaving me
to keep on drinking
just me
sitting there
then the face of the
bartender near
mine:

"LAST CALL!"

his meaty indifferent face
cheap in the cheap
light

to have my last drink
go out to my ten year old car
at the curb
get in
to drive ever so carefully
to my rented
room

remembering the schoolyard
again,
recess time,
being chosen next to last
on the baseball team,
the same sun shining on me
as on them,
now it was night,
most people of the world
together.
my cigarette dangling,
I heard the sound of the
engine.

the editor

he sat in the kitchen   at the breakfastnook table
reading the manuscripts   writing a short rejection
on each   replacing the paperclip   then
sliding the pages   back into   the brown
manila envelopes.

he'd been reading   for an hour and thirty-five
minutes   and hadn't found a single poem

well   he'd have to   do the usual thing
for the next issue: write the poems himself and
make up names   for the authors.

where was   the talent?

for the last 3 decades   the poets had
flattened
out   it was like reading   stuff
from a house of
subnormals.

but
he'd save   Rabowski
for last

Rabowski had sent 8 or ten poems in a batch
but always   there were one or two
good ones.

he sighed   and pulled out the Rabowski
poems.

he slowly read them   he finished

he got up   went to the refrigerator
got out

a can of beer   cracked it   sat back
down

he read the poems all over again   they were
all bad   even Rabowski had
crapped out.

the editor got out a printed rejection slip
wrote   "you must have had a bad
week."
then he slipped the poems back into the
manila envelope   sealed it   tossed it
on top of the pile   for mailing

then he took the beer   sat down next to his wife
on the couch

she was watching Johnny Carson
he watched

Carson was bad   Carson knew he was bad   but
he couldn't do anything about
it.

the editor got up   with his can of beer   and
began walking up the
stairway.

"where are you going?" his wife
asked.

"to bed   to sleep."

"but   it's early."

"god damn it   I know that!"

"well   you needn't act *that way*
about it!"

he walked into the bedroom   flicked on
the wall switch
there was a small bright flash and then
the overhead light burned
out.

he sat on the edge of the bed   and finished his
beer   in the
dark.

duck and forget it

today at the track
I was standing alone
looking down
when I saw these
two shoes
moving directly
toward
me

at once
I started into motion
toward my right
but he still caught part of
me:

"making any money
today?"

"yeah," I answered and
was gone.

not too many years ago
I would have stood
there
while this slipped
soul
unloaded his
inanities on
me
pissing over my day
and my feelings
as he made me pay
for where he allowed
himself to be
in his mind
and in his
life.

no longer.

yet I am my brother's
keeper.

I keep him
away.

snapshots at the track

I go to the men's crapper
for a bowel
movement,
get up to flush.
what the hell.
something blood-dark
falls upon the
seat.
I'm 70, I
drink.
have been on my deathbed
twice.
I reach down for what has
fallen . . .
it's a small burnt
potato chip
from my
lunch.
not yet . . .
damn thing fell from my
shirt . . .

I finish my toiletry,
go out and watch the
race.
my horse runs
second
chasing a 25-to-one
shot
to the
wire.

I don't mind.

then I see this fellow
rushing toward me,
he always needs a
shave, his glasses seem

about to fall off
his face,
he knows me
and maybe I know
him.

"hey, Hank, Hank!"

we shake hands like two
lost souls.
"always good to see you,"
he says, "it refreshes
me, I know you lead a
hard life
just like I
do."

"sure, kid, how you
doing?"

he tells me that he is
a big winner
then
rushes off.
the big board
overhead
flashes the first odds
on the next
race.

I check my program
decide to leave the
clubhouse,
try my luck in the
grandstand,
that's where a hard-
living player belongs
anyhow,
right?

right.

x-idol

I never watch tv so I don't know
but I'm told he was the leading man in a
long-running
series.
he does movie bits
now
I see him at the track almost every
day ("I used to have women coming out of
my ass," he once informed me).
and people still remember him, call him
by name and my wife often asks me, "did
you see him today?"
"oh yes, he's a gambling son of a bitch."

the track is where you go when the other
action drops away.

he still looks like a celebrity, the way
he walks and talks and
I never meet him without feeling
good.

the toteboard flashes.

the sky shakes.

the mountains call us home.

heat wave

another one.
this night the people sit drunk or drugged or some of them
sit in front of their tv sets
slapped silly.
some few have air-conditioning.

the neighborhood dogs and cats flop about
waiting for a better time.

and I remember the cars along the freeway today
some of them stalled in the fast lane,
hoods up.

there are more murders in the heat
more domestic arguments.

Los Angeles has been burning for
weeks.

even the desperately lonely have not phoned
and that alone
makes all this almost
worthwhile:

those little mewling voices cooked into
silence
as I listen to the music of a long dead man
written in the 19th
century.

we ain't got no money, honey, but we got rain

call it the greenhouse effect or whatever
but it just doesn't rain like it
used to.

I particularly remember the rains of the
depression era.
there wasn't any money but there was
plenty of rain.

it wouldn't rain for just a night or
a day,
it would RAIN for 7 days and 7
nights
and in Los Angeles the storm drains
weren't built to carry off that much
water
and the rain came down THICK and
MEAN and
STEADY
and you HEARD it banging against
the roofs and into the ground
waterfalls of it came down
from the roofs
and often there was HAIL
big ROCKS OF ICE
bombing
exploding
smashing into things
and the rain
just wouldn't
STOP
and all the roofs leaked—
dishpans,
cooking pots
were placed all about;
they dripped loudly
and had to be emptied

again and
again.

the rain came up over the street curbings,
across the lawns, climbed the steps and
entered the houses.
there were mops and bathroom towels,
and the rain often came up through the
toilets: bubbling, brown, crazy, whirling,
and the old cars stood in the streets,
cars that had problems starting on a
sunny day,
and the jobless men stood
looking out the windows
at the old machines dying
like living things
out there.

the jobless men,
failures in a failing time
were imprisoned in their houses with their
wives and children
and their
pets.
the pets refused to go out
and left their waste in
strange places.

the jobless men went mad
confined with
their once beautiful wives.
there were terrible arguments
as notices of foreclosure
fell into the mailbox.
rain and hail, cans of beans,
bread without butter; fried
eggs, boiled eggs, poached
eggs; peanut butter
sandwiches, and an invisible

chicken
in every pot.

my father, never a good man
at best, beat my mother
when it rained
as I threw myself
between them,
the legs, the knees, the
screams
until they
separated.

"*I'll kill you,*" I screamed
at him. "*You hit her again
and I'll kill you!*"

"*Get that son-of-a-bitching
kid out of here!*"

"no, Henry, you stay with
your mother!"

all the households were under
siege but I believe that ours
held more terror than the
average.

and at night
as we attempted to sleep
the rains still came down
and it was in bed
in the dark
watching the moon against
the scarred window
so bravely
holding out
most of the rain,
I thought of Noah and the
Ark

and I thought, it has come
again.
we all thought
that.

and then, at once, it would
stop.
and it always seemed to
stop
around 5 or 6 a.m.,
peaceful then,
but not an exact silence
because things continued to
drip
      drip
           drip

and there was no smog then
and by 8 a.m.
there was a
blazing yellow sunlight,
Van Gogh yellow—
crazy, blinding!
and then
the roof drains
relieved of the rush of
water
began to expand in
the warmth:
PANG! PANG! PANG!

and everybody got up
and looked outside
and there were all the lawns
still soaked
greener than green will ever
be
and there were the birds
on the lawn
CHIRPING like mad,

they hadn't eaten decently
for 7 days and 7 nights
and they were weary of
berries
and
they waited as the worms
rose to the top,
half-drowned worms.
the birds plucked them
up
and gobbled them
down; there were
blackbirds and sparrows.
the blackbirds tried to
drive the sparrows off
but the sparrows,
maddened with hunger,
smaller and quicker,
got their
due.

the men stood on their porches
smoking cigarettes,
now knowing
they'd have to go out
there
to look for that job
that probably wasn't
there, to start that car
that probably wouldn't
start.

and the once beautiful
wives
stood in their bathrooms
combing their hair,
applying makeup,
trying to put their world back
together again,
trying to forget that

awful sadness that
gripped them,
wondering what they could
fix for
breakfast.

and on the radio
we were told that
school was now
open.
and
soon
there I was
on the way to school,
massive puddles in the
street,
the sun like a new
world,
my parents back in that
house,
I arrived at my classroom
on time.

Mrs. Sorenson greeted us
with, "we won't have our
usual recess, the grounds
are too wet."

"AW!" most of the boys
went.

"but we are going to do
something special at
recess," she went on,
"and it will be
fun!"

well, we all wondered
what that would
be

and the two hour wait
seemed a long time
as Mrs. Sorenson
went about
teaching her
lessons.

I looked at the little
girls, they all looked so
pretty and clean and
alert,
they sat still and
straight
and their hair was
beautiful
in the California
sunshine.

then the recess bell rang
and we all waited for the
fun.

then Mrs. Sorenson told
us:
"now, what we are going to
do is we are going to tell
each other what we did
during the rainstorm!
we'll begin in the front
row and go right around!
now, Michael, you're
first! . . ."

well, we all began to tell
our stories, Michael began
and it went on and on,
and soon we realized that
we were all lying, not
exactly lying but mostly
lying and some of the boys

began to snicker and some
of the girls began to give
them dirty looks and
Mrs. Sorenson said,
"all right, I demand a
modicum of silence
here!
I am interested in what
you did
during the rainstorm
even if you
aren't!"

so we had to tell our
stories and they *were*
stories.

one girl said that
when the rainbow first
came
she saw God's face
at the end of it.
only she didn't say
which end.

one boy said he stuck
his fishing pole
out the window
and caught a little
fish
and fed it to his
cat.

almost everybody told
a lie.
the truth was just
too awful and
embarrassing to
tell.

then the bell rang
and recess was
over.

"thank you," said Mrs.
Sorenson, "that was very
nice.
and tomorrow the grounds
will be dry
and we will put them
to use
again."

most of the boys
cheered
and the little girls
sat very straight and
still,
looking so pretty and
clean and
alert,
their hair beautiful
in a sunshine that
the world might
never see
again.

crime and punishment

Mr. Sanderson was the principal of
my high school
and it seemed that much
of the time
I was in Mr. Sanderson's
office
and I had no idea
why.

the teacher would send me down
with a sealed
envelope.
Mr. Sanderson would open the
envelope
read the enclosure
and then look at
me.

"well, here we are
again!
we just *can't* behave our-
selves, can
we?"

he always said the same
thing.
I rather liked the idea of
being bad
but I had no idea
that I
was.

I didn't protest
because
I thought that
the teachers were
stupid

and that
Mr. Sanderson was
stupid
so
there was nobody
to protest
to.
certainly not
my parents
who were more stupid
than
any of
them.

"all right," Mr. Sanderson would
say, "go into the phone booth,
close the door
and don't come out until I
tell you
to."

it was one of those
glassed in phone booths with a
little seat.
all the times I sat there
the phone never
rang.
and it was stuffy
in there.
all you could do in there
was think
and I didn't want to
think.
Mr. Sanderson knew that.
there were magazines in
there
but they were all dull,
fancy ladies
magazines
but I read them

anyhow
and that really made me
feel bad
which was what Mr.
Sanderson wanted.

finally
after one or two hours
he would bang on the
door with his big
fist and yell, "ALL RIGHT,
YOU CAN COME OUT OF THERE
NOW
AND I DON'T EVER WANT TO
SEE YOU IN HERE AGAIN!"

but
I'd be back
many times

never knowing
why.

finally
like somebody doing
time
I got out of that
high school
and it was a couple
of years later
that I read
in the newspaper
that Mr. Sanderson
had been
prosecuted
fined and
jailed
for
embezzlement of

school
funds.

while I had been
in that phone booth
diddling with
myself
that son of a
bitch
had been making
his
moves.

I felt like
going down to
the jail
and dumping a
bunch of
Ladies' Home Journal
on him
but of course
I didn't.
I felt good enough
about it
just the way it
was.

the soldier, his wife and the bum

I was a bum in San Francisco but once managed
to go to a symphony concert along with the well-
dressed people
and the music was good but something about the
audience was not
and something about the orchestra
and the conductor was
not,
although the building was fine and the
acoustics perfect
I preferred to listen to the music alone
on my radio
and afterwards I did go back to my room and I
turned on the radio but
then there was a pounding on the wall:
"SHUT THAT GOD-DAMNED THING OFF!"

there was a soldier in the next room
living with his wife
and he would soon be going over there to pro-
tect me from Hitler so
I snapped the radio off and then heard his
wife say, "you shouldn't have done that."
and the soldier said, "FUCK THAT GUY!"
which I thought was a very nice thing for him
to tell his wife to do.
of course,
she never did.

anyhow, I never went to another live concert
and that night I listened to the radio very
quietly, my ear pressed to the
speaker.

war has its price and peace never lasts and
millions of young men everywhere would die
and as I listened to the classical music I

heard them making love, desperately and
mournfully, through Shostakovich, Brahms,
Mozart, through crescendo and climax,
and through the shared
wall of our darkness.

Bonaparte's Retreat

Fred, they called him.
he always sat at the end of the
bar
near the doorway
and he was always there
from opening to
closing.
he was there more than
I was,
which is saying
something.

he never talked to
anybody.
he just sat there
drinking his glasses of
draft beer.
he looked straight ahead
right across the bar
but he never looked at
anybody.

and there's one other
thing.

he got up
now and then
and went to the
jukebox
and he always played the
same record:
Bonaparte's Retreat.

he played that song
all day and all night
long.

it was his song,
all right.

he never got tired
of it.

and when his draft beers
really got to him
he'd get up and play
Bonaparte's Retreat
6 or 7 times
running.

nobody knew who he was or
how he made
it,
only that he lived in a
hotel room
across the street
and was the first customer
in the bar
each day
as it
opened.

I protested to Clyde
the bartender:
"listen, he's driving us
crazy with that
thing.
eventually, all the other
records are
rotated
but
Bonaparte's Retreat
remains.
what does it
mean?"

"it's his song,"
said Clyde.

"don't you have a
song?"

well, I came in about one
p.m. this day
and all the regulars
were there
but Fred wasn't
there.

I ordered my drink,
then said out loud,
"hey, where's
Fred?"

"Fred's dead,"
said Clyde.

I looked down at the end
of the bar.
the sun came through the
blinds
but there was nobody
at the end
stool.

"you're kidding me,"
I said, "Fred's back in the
crapper or
something."

"Fred didn't come in this
morning," said Clyde, "so
I went over to his
hotel room
and there he
was
stiff as a
cigar
box."

everybody was very
quiet.
those guys never said
much
anyhow.

"well," I said, "at least
we won't have to hear
Bonaparte's Retreat
anymore."

nobody said
anything.

"is that record
still in the
juke?" I
asked.

"yes," said
Clyde.

"well," I said,
"I'm going to play it
one more time."

I got up.

"hold it,"
said Clyde.

he came around the bar,
walked to the
juke
box.

he had a little key
in his
hand.

he put the key
in the juke
and opened
it.

he reached in
and pulled
out a
record.

then he took the
record and
broke it over
his
knee.

"it was his
song," said
Clyde.

then he locked
the juke,
took the broken
record
behind the bar
and
trashed
it.

the name of the
bar
was
Jewel's.
it was at
Crenshaw and
Adams
and it's not
there
anymore.

flat tire

got a flat on the freeway
11 a.m.
going north
I got over to the
side
a small strip
on the freeway
edge
got out the jack
and the
spare
went to
work
the big rigs
going by
blasts of air and
noise
shaking everything
and to top it
all
it was
cold
an icy
wind
and I thought,
Jesus Christ, mercy,
can I do this
thing?
this would be a
good place to
go crazy and
chuck it all
in

but I got the
new wheel
on,

the old one
in the trunk
and then I was
back in the
car

I gunned it into
the swirl of
traffic
and there I was
like nothing
had ever
happened

moving along
with everybody
else

all of us
caught up in our
petty larcenies
and our
rotting
virtues

I gunned it
hard
made the fast
lane

pushed the
button
as my radio
antenna
sliced into the
sky.

oh, I was a ladies' man!

you
wonder about
the time
when
you ran through women
like an open-field
maniac
with this total
disregard for
panties, dish towels,
photos
and all the other
accoutrements—
like
the tangling of
souls.

what
were you
trying to
do
trying to
catch up
with?

it was like a
hunt.
how many
could you
bag?
move
onto?

names
shoes
dresses
sheets, bathrooms

bedrooms, kitchens
back
rooms,
cafes,
pets,
names of pets,
names of children;
middle names, last
names, made-up
names.

you proved it was
easy.
you proved it
could be done
again and
again,
those legs held
high
behind most of
you.
or
they were on top
or
you were
behind
or
both
sideways
plus
other
inventions.

songs on radios.
parked cars.
telephone voices.
the pouring of
drinks.
the senseless
conversations.

now you know
you were nothing but a
fucking
dog,
a snail wrapped around
a snail—
sticky shells in the
sunlight, or in
the misty evenings,
or in the dark
dark.

you were
nature's
idiot,
not proving but
being
proved.
not a man but a
plan
unfolding,
not thrusting but
being
pierced.
now
you know.

then
you thought you were
such a
clever devil
such a
cad
such a
man-bull
such a
bad boy

smiling over your
wine

planning your next
move

what a
waste of time
you were

you great
rider
you Attila of
the springs and
elsewhere

you could have
slept through it
all
and you would never
have been
missed

never would have
been
missed
at
all.

inactive volcano

the bartender at Musso's
remembers me when
I was
in rags,
used to
lean on the wood
with the
worst and loudest of
women
and
we would
drink too much
spill our drinks
get
nasty.

now
I enter
quietly with an
interviewer
a film director
or some
actor
or
with my wife
and a gentle
friend or
two.

at times
now
I see the bartender
looking at me
and I know
he's thinking
of back then
the way it

was
and I look
back at him
and my eyes
send the
message:
I'm just the
same, friend, only
the circumstances
have
altered
but
I'm
the same.

then I
turn back
to
whomever
I am with
and they
too
seem to be
thinking,
when is he
going to go
crazy
again?

nothing
to do,
friend,
but
wait
and
see.

creative writing class

I'm guilty, I did take one
in college
and the first thing I realized was that
I could beat the hell out of any
2 or 3 people in there
at once
(physically
I mean)
and
of course
this was no way to measure
creativity.

also
I noticed that the professor's advice
on what to do
and what not to do
to become a writer was
very pale and standard stuff
that would lead to
nowhere.

some of the students' work
was read in class
and I found it to be embarrassingly
inept.

I sat alone in the back row with
my scowl
further noting that
the men didn't look like men and
the women didn't look like women.
again
no way to judge creativity.
but what they produced
looked like
what they were.

well
at least the prof did give me
"A's" on all the work
I turned in
but I got a "B" overall for
poor attendance.

I also knew that
every student in that class
except one
was
creatively doomed.

and even that one
would be 50 years old
before even minor notice
would be taken of
his work.

a bit longer
than even he
had
expected.

cool black air

often from my typing room I step out onto this small
balcony
and there is the night
a cool wash of black air.
I stand in slippers, shorts and undershirt, sucking at
a small cigarette, I can see the curling headlights of
the cars on the winding Harbor Freeway.
they come and come, those lights, they never stop
and I truly wonder that life is still here
after all these centuries, after the hell of
all of our error and our smallness and our
greed, our
selfishness, our bitterness,
life is still here
and the thought of that makes me strangely
elated.
of course, I am woozy from hours of
typing.

and now
the same dog in that yard to the far left barks at me
again.

he should know that old fart standing there in his shorts,
he should know me by now.

I turn and walk back into my typing room.

the typewriter is electric and it is on and it
hums hums hums hums.

last night I did something very odd: after ripping out
a few poems
I covered the machine
then bent down and kissed it once, and said,
"thank you, very much."

after 50 years in the game I had finally thanked my
typewriter.

now I sit down to it and I BANG IT, I don't use the light
touch, I BANG IT, I want to hear it, I want it to do its
tricks, it has saved my ass from the worst of women and the
worst of men and the
worst of jobs, it has mellowed my nightmares into a gentle
sanity, it has loved me at my lowest and it has made me
seem to be a greater soul than I ever
was.

I BANG IT   I BANG IT

and I know how all of them felt, all the writers, when it was
going good, when it was going hot.

death, I have chopped off your arms and your legs and your
head.

I am sorry, I know you just do what you have to
do

even to that barking dog

but now
I BANG IT
BANG IT

and wait.

the jackals

as the years went on I seemed to have more luck
but now these jackals
these attackers from the past reappear as if
nothing had ever
occurred (one doesn't mind literary
criticism so long as the envy and the rancor
do not show through)
and now I meet the jackals in eating
places etc.
some even come to the door
bringing entire families—mothers, fathers,
old aunts . . .

the jackals turn on the charm
and I don't mind, let the past be
done, I pour the drinks and
listen.

it is afterwards that it occurs, usually
within a week:
a large manuscript arrives with
note: "could you read this?
publisher would like a foreword from
you . . ."

I brace myself, flop on the bed, give it
a read: the writing is proficient
but somewhere there is a terrible
lacking, an unnatural void . . .
the manuscript makes me a bit ill;
I let it fall to the
floor.

the other night I made a brief
appearance at a theater where my
video was showing and

as I was leaving
here came the poet, glass of
cheap free wine in his hand, he
poked his face into mine
and repeated his *same* speech all
over again as if he had forgotten
he had given it
to me before.

"remember me? we met at L's.
there's this new mag starting, it's
going to be better than *Rolling
Stone* . . .
what they want me to do is
interview you and you interview me,
we get a thousand a-piece, maybe
more . . ."

(said jackal had attacked me in an
article after begging me to go
to the boxing matches with him.
his face was continually
in mine, talking, talking.
"listen," I told him, "let's just
watch the fights . . ."
he had told
me he was there to cover the
fights, but he wasn't: the
article was about me: a
terrible human being who was a
drunk and far past his prime.)

now he kept shoving his face into
mine there on the sidewalk,
repeating his spiel: "I interview
you, you interview me . . . one
thousand, what do you think, huh,
huh?"

"I'll let you know," I told
him.

but he just kept walking along,
pushing his face into mine . . .

well, I thought, I am going to
have to punch him out.

but I tried something else
first:

"get the fuck away from me!"

he backed off and I walked off
to a better place . . .

give it a week, I came in from the
track one evening and here was a
large package: 3 of his latest
books from a local press.
I flipped through the pages:
a breezy, bantering style
playing the open, good
human guy but it was like he
was writing on benzedrine
lashing you with shreds of his
soul,
but it was more boring-
than derring-
do.

there was a note with phone
number, home address:
"I'll interview you, you
interview me, the editor thinks
it's a great idea . . . and there's a
grand a-piece in it for each of
us, maybe more . . ."

I walked into the kitchen and
dumped him into the trash
bag.

I fed the cats and then the phone
rang.
it was a new voice:

"Chinaski?"

"yes?"

"listen, you don't know me
but my name is Dipper
and I got a great deal for
you."

"listen, how did you get my
phone number?"

"hey, man, what difference
does *that* make?"

I hung up.

in a moment the phone was ringing
again.

I walked into the front room
looked out the south window, it
looked fine out there: trees, lawn,
shrubbery,
not a jackal in
sight.

warm light

alone
tonight
in this house,
alone with
6 cats
who tell me
without
effort
all that there
is
to know.

4

in the shadow of the rose

Dinosauria, we

born like this
into this
as the chalk faces smile
as Mrs. Death laughs
as the elevators break
as political landscapes dissolve
as the supermarket bag boy holds a college degree
as the oily fish spit out their oily prey
as the sun is masked

we are
born like this
into this
into these carefully mad wars
into the sight of broken factory windows of emptiness
into bars where people no longer speak to each other
into fist fights that end as shootings and knifings

born into this
into hospitals which are so expensive that it's cheaper to die
into lawyers who charge so much it's cheaper to plead guilty
into a country where the jails are full and the madhouses closed
into a place where the masses elevate fools into rich heroes

born into this
walking and living through this
dying because of this
muted because of this
castrated
debauched
disinherited
because of this
fooled by this
used by this
pissed on by this
made crazy and sick by this
made violent

made inhuman
by this

the heart is blackened
the fingers reach for the throat
the gun
the knife
the bomb
the fingers reach toward an unresponsive god

the fingers reach for the bottle
the pill
the powder

we are born into this sorrowful deadliness
we are born into a government 60 years in debt
that soon will be unable to even pay the interest on that debt
and the banks will burn
money will be useless
there will be open and unpunished murder in the streets
it will be guns and roving mobs
land will be useless
food will become a diminishing return
nuclear power will be taken over by the many
explosions will continually shake the earth
radiated robot men will stalk each other
the rich and the chosen will watch from space platforms
Dante's Inferno will be made to look like a children's playground

the sun will not be seen and it will always be night
trees will die
all vegetation will die
radiated men will eat the flesh of radiated men
the sea will be poisoned
the lakes and rivers will vanish
rain will be the new gold

the rotting bodies of men and animals will stink in the dark wind

the last few survivors will be overtaken by new and hideous diseases

and the space platforms will be destroyed by attrition
the petering out of supplies
the natural effect of general decay

and there will be the most beautiful silence never heard

born out of that.

the sun still hidden there

awaiting the next chapter.

cut while shaving

It's never quite right, he said, the way the people look,
the way the music sounds, the way the words are
written.
it's never quite right, he said, all the things we are
taught, all the loves we chase, all the deaths we
die, all the lives we live,
they are never quite right,
they are hardly close to right,
these lives we live
one after the other,
piled there as history,
the waste of the species,
the crushing of the light and the way,
it's not quite right,
it's hardly right at all
he said.

don't I know it? I
answered.

I walked away from the mirror.
it was morning, it was afternoon, it was
night

nothing changed
it was locked in place.
something flashed, something broke, something
remained.

I walked down the stairway and
into it.

a good job

some jobs you like,
there is a clean gentle
feel to some of them,
like the one I had
unloading boxcars
of frozen
fish.

the fish came packed
in coffin-sized boxes,
beautifully
heavy and
almost
unyielding.
you had thick gloves
and a hook
and you gaffed the
damned thing
and pulled it along
the floor and slid it
outside and onto the
waiting
truck.

and strangely there
was no foreman,
they just turned us
loose in there
knowing we'd get
it done.

we were always
sending out one of
the fellows for another
bottle of
wine.
it was slippery and

cold in those
boxcars

we yanked out those
iced fish,
drank the wine
and the bullshit
flew.
there was a
fight or two
but nothing really
violent.
I was the peace-
maker.

"come on, fuck
that stuff!
let's get these
fish out of
here!
yeah!"

then we'd be
laughing and
bullshitting
again.

toward evening
we all got quiet.
the fish seemed to
get heavier and
heavier.
shins got cracked,
knees
bruised
and the wine
settled heavily
into our
guts.

by the time you
got to your last box
you bullied it
out of there
strictly on nerve
alone.

when you punched
out
even the timecard
seemed
heavy.

and then you were
in your old car
moving toward
your place,
your shackjob,
wondering
whether good times
or hell
awaited
you.

but the frozen fish
you had
worked,
that thought was
pleasant and
soothing,
and you'd be back
for more,
hooking the wood
and dragging.

the night came
on and you flicked
the headlights
on

and the world was
good enough,
right
then.

last seat at the end

I was always studying the wood of the
bar, the grains, the scratches, the
cigarette burns.
there was something there but I
couldn't quite figure what it
was
and that kept me going.

another one was to look at my
hand around the
glass.
there is something about
one's hand about a
glass that is gently
fascinating.

and, of course, there is this one:
all drunks do it:
taking your thumbnail and slowly
ripping off the label
on a bottle of beer that has been
soaking in the icewater.

smoking cigarettes is a good show
too, especially in the early morning
hours with the Venetian blinds at
your back,
the smoke curls up and forms its
divergent patterns.
this gives one the feeling of
peace
and really so, more so,
if there is one of your favorite
old songs
emanating from the
juke.

and if the bartender was old
and a little tired and a little bit
wise
it was good to see where he
was or what he was doing—
washing glasses or leaning
against the counter or
sneaking a quick
shot
or whatever he was doing
it was always nice to just
see a bit of him,
to take note of the white
shirt.
the white shirt was an
important backdrop to
drink to and
with.

also you listened to the
traffic going by,
car by car.
it was not a deliberate
listening—more an off-
hand
one.
and it was best when
it had rained
and you could hear the
tires on the
wet street.

the bar was the best
place to hide in.
time came under your
control, time to wade
in, time to do nothing
in.

no guru was needed,
no god.

nothing expected but
yourself
and nothing lost
to the
unexpected.

my uncle Jack

my uncle Jack
is a mouse
is a house on fire
is a war about to begin
is a man running down the street with a knife in his back.

my uncle Jack
is the Santa Monica pier
is a dusty blue pillow
is a scratching black-and-white dog
is a man with one arm lighting a cigarette with one hand.

my uncle Jack
is a slice of burnt toast
is the place you forgot to look for the key
is the pleasure of finding 3 rolls of toilet paper in the closet
is the worst dream you've ever had that you can't remember.

my uncle Jack
is the firecracker that went off in your hand
is your run-over cat dead outside your driveway at 10:30 a.m.
is the crap game you won in the Santa Anita parking lot
is the man your woman left you for that night in the cheap hotel
    room.

my uncle Jack
is your uncle Jack
is death coming like a freight train
is a clown with weeping eyes
is your car jack and your fingernails and the scream of the biggest
    mountain now.

the area of pause

you have to have it or the walls will close
in.
you have to give everything up, throw it
away, everything away.
you have to look at what you look at
or think what you think
or do what you do
or
don't do
without considering personal
advantage
without accepting guidance.

people are worn away with
striving,
they hide in common
habits.
their concerns are herd
concerns.

few have the ability to stare
at an old shoe for
ten minutes
or to think of odd things
like who invented the
doorknob?

they become unalive
because they are unable to
pause
undo themselves
unkink
unsee
unlearn
roll clear.

listen to their untrue
laughter, then
walk
away.

my first computer poem

have I gone the way of the deathly death?
will this machine finish me
where booze and women and poverty
have not?

is Whitman laughing at me from his grave?
does Creeley care?

is this properly spaced?
am I?

will Ginsberg howl?

soothe me!

get me lucky!

get me good!

get me going!

I am a virgin again.

a 70 year old virgin.

don't fuck me, machine

do.
who cares?

talk to me, machine!

we can drink together.
we can have fun.

think of all the people who will hate me at this
computer.

we'll add them to the others
and continue right
on.

so this is the beginning
not the
end.

Rossini, Mozart and Shostakovich

are who I will hear tonight
after reading about the death of Red Grange.
my wife and I ate at a Japanese restaurant tonight
and I told her that Red Grange had died.
I had red bean ice cream for dessert.
my wife declined.
the war was still on in the Gulf.
we got into the car and I drove us back here.
now I am listening to Rossini
who died before Red Grange.
now the audience is applauding.
now the players are readying for Mozart.
Red Grange got a hell of a write-up in the papers.
now Mozart is beginning.
I am smoking a small cigarette imported from India.
4 of my 6 cats are asleep in the next room.
my wife is downstairs.
outside it is a cold, still winter night.
I blow smoke into the desk lamp and watch it curl.
Mozart is doing very well.
Shostakovich is getting ready.
it is a late Tuesday evening.
and Red Grange is dead.

it's a shame

a great mind and a good body seldom go
together.
or a great body and a good
mind.
or a great body and a great
mind.

but worse, a not so good mind and a
not so good body often go
together.

in fact, that's almost the entire
populace.
and all these
reproducing more of
themselves.

is there any wonder why the world
is where it's at
now?

just notice the creature sitting near you
in a movie house
or standing ahead of you in a
supermarket line.
or giving a State of the Union
Address.

that the gods have let us go on
this long
this badly.

as the snail comes crawling home
to manna.

what a writer

what I liked about e. e. cummings
was that he cut away from
the holiness of the
word
and with charm
and gamble
gave us lines
that sliced through the
dung.

how it was needed!
how we were withering
away
in the old
tired
manner.

of course, then came all
the
e. e. cummings
copyists.
they copied him then
as the others had
copied Keats, Shelley,
Swinburne, Byron, et
al.

but there was only
one
e. e. cummings.
of course.

one sun.

one moon.

one poet,
like
that.

hangovers

I've probably had about more of them
than any person alive
and they haven't killed me
yet
but some of those mornings felt
awfully near
death.

as you know, the worst drinking is done
on an empty stomach, while smoking
heavily and downing many different
types of
libations.

and the worst hangovers are when you
awaken in your car or in a strange room
or in an alley or in jail.

the worst hangovers are when you
awaken to realize that you have done
something absolutely vile, ignorant and
possibly dangerous the night before
but
you can't quite remember what it
was.

and you awaken in various states of
disorder—parts of your body
damaged, your money missing
and/or possibly and often your
car, if you had one.

you might place a telephone call to
a lady, if you were with one, most
often to have her slam the phone
down on you.
or, if she is next to you then,

to feel her bristling and outrageous
anger.

drunks are never forgiven.

but drunks will forgive themselves
because they need to drink
again.

it takes an ungodly durability to
be a drinking person for many
decades.

your drinking companions are
killed by it.
you yourself are in and out of
hospitals
where the warning often is:
"One more drink will kill
you."
but
you beat that
by taking more than one more
drink.

and as you near three quarters of
a century in age
you find that it takes more and more
booze to get you
drunk.

and the hangovers are worse,
the recovery stage is
longer.

and the most remarkably stupid
thing is
that you are not unpleased that
you have done it
all

and that you are still
doing it.

I am typing this now
under the yoke of one of my
worst hangovers
while downstairs now
sit various and sundry
bottles of
alcohol.

it's all been so beastly
lovely,
this mad river,
this gouging
plundering
madness
that I would wish upon
nobody
but myself,
amen.

they are everywhere

the tragedy-sniffers are all
about.
they get up in the morning
and begin to find things
wrong
and they fling themselves
into a rage about
it,
a rage that lasts until
bedtime,
where even there
they twist in their
insomnia,
not able to rid their
minds
of the petty obstacles
they have
encountered.

they feel set against,
it's a plot.
and by being constantly
angry they feel that
they are constantly
right.

you see them in traffic
honking wildly
at the slightest
infraction,
cursing,
spewing their
invectives.

you feel them
in lines
at banks

at supermarkets
at movies,
they are pressing
at your back
walking on your
heels,
they are impatient to
a fury.

they are everywhere
and into
everything,
these violently
unhappy
souls.

actually they are
frightened,
never wanting to be
wrong
they lash out
incessantly . . .
it is a malady
an illness of
that
breed.

the first one
I saw like that
was my
father

and since then
I have seen a
thousand
fathers,
ten thousand
fathers
wasting their lives
in hatred,

tossing their lives
into the
cesspool
and
ranting
on.

war

war, war, war,
the yellow monster,
the eater of mind
and body.
war,
the indescribable,
the pleasure of
the mad,
the final argument
of
ungrown men.

does it belong?

do we?

as we approach
the last flash of
our chance.

one flower left.

one second.

breathing like this.

the idiot

I believe the thought came to me
when I was about eleven years
old:
   I'll become an idiot.

I had noticed some in the neigh-
borhood,
those who the people called
"idiots."

although looked down upon,
the idiots seemed to have the
more peaceful lives:
nothing was expected of
them.

I imagined myself standing upon
streetcorners, hands in pockets,
and drooling a bit at the
mouth.

nobody would bother
me.

I began to put my plan into
effect.

I was first noticed in the
school yards.
my mates jibed at me,
taunted me.

even my father noticed:
"you act like a god damned
idiot!"

one of my teachers noticed,
Mrs. Gredis of the long silken
legs.

she kept me after
class.

"what is it, Henry?
you can tell me . . ."

she put her arms
about me
and I rested myself
against
her.

"tell me, Henry, don't
be afraid . . ."

I didn't say
anything.

"you can stay here
as long as you
want, Henry.
you don't have to
talk . . ."

she kissed me on the
forehead
and I reached down
and lightly touched
one of her silken
legs.

Mrs. Gredis was a
hot number.

she kept me after
school almost every
day.

and everybody hated
me
but I believe that I
had the most wonderful
hard-ons
of any eleven year old
boy
in the city of
Los Angeles

this rejoinder

the people survive to come up with flat fists full
of nothing.
I remember Carl Sandburg's poem, "The
People, Yes."
nice thought but completely inaccurate:
the people did not survive through a noble
strength but through lie, compromise and
guile.
I lived with these people, I am not so sure
what people Sandburg lived
with.
but his poem always pissed me off.
it was a poem that lied.
it is "The People, No."
then and now.
and it doesn't take a misanthrope to
say this.

let us hope that future famous poems
such as Mr. Sandburg's
make more
sense.

Hemingway never did this

I read that he lost a suitcase full of manuscripts on a
train and that they never were recovered.
I can't match the agony of this
but the other night I wrote a 3-page poem
upon this computer
and through my lack of diligence and
practice
and by playing around with commands
on the menu
I somehow managed to erase the poem
forever.
believe me, such a thing is difficult to do
even for a novice
but I somehow managed to do
it.

now I don't think this 3-pager was immor-
tal
but there were some crazy wild lines,
now gone forever.
it bothers more than a touch, it's some-
thing like knocking over a good bottle of
wine.

and writing about it hardly makes a good
poem.
still, I thought somehow you'd like to
know?

if not, at least you've read this far
and there could be better work
down the line.

let's hope so, for your sake
and
mine.

surprise time again

it's always a surprise to some
when the killer is that clean-cut
quiet boy with the gentle smile
who went to church
and was nearly a straight-A
student
and also good on the athletic
field,
kind to his elders,
adored by the young girls,
the old ones,
admired by his
peers.

"I can't believe he did it . . ."

they always think a killer must
be ugly, gross, unlikable,
that he must give off signs,
signals of anger and
madness.

sometimes these kill
too.

but a potential killer can never
be judged by his
externals

nor a politician, a priest or
a poet.

or the dog
or the woman
wagging
tails.

the killer sits anywhere
like you
as you read this

wondering.

young in New Orleans

starving there, sitting around the bars,
and at night walking the streets for
hours,
the moonlight always seemed fake
to me, maybe it was,
and in the French Quarter I watched
the horses and buggies going by,
everybody sitting high in the open
carriages, the black driver, and in
back the man and the woman,
usually young and always white.
and I was always white.
and hardly charmed by the
world.
New Orleans was a place to
hide.
I could piss away my life,
unmolested.
except for the rats.
the rats in my dark small room
very much resented sharing it
with me.
they were large and fearless
and stared at me with eyes
that spoke
an unblinking
death.

women were beyond me.
they saw something
depraved.
there was one waitress
a little older than
I, she rather smiled,
lingered when she
brought my
coffee.

that was plenty for
me, that was
enough.

there was something about
that city, though:
it didn't let me feel guilty
that I had no feeling for the
things so many others
needed.
it let me alone.

sitting up in my bed
the lights out,
hearing the outside
sounds,
lifting my cheap
bottle of wine,
letting the warmth of
the grape
enter
me
as I heard the rats
moving about the
room,
I preferred them
to
humans.

being lost,
being crazy maybe
is not so bad
if you can be
that way:
undisturbed.

New Orleans gave me
that.
nobody ever called
my name.

no telephone,
no car,
no job,
no
anything.

me and the
rats
and my youth,
one time,
that time
I knew
even through the
nothingness,
it was a
celebration
of something not to
do
but only
know.

the damnation of Buk

getting old, and older, concerned that
you might not get your driver's license
renewed, concerned that the hangovers
last longer, concerned that you might
not reach the age of 85,
concerned that the poems will stop
arriving.
concerned that you are concerned.

concerned that you might die in the
spa.
concerned that you might die on the
freeway while driving in from the
track.
concerned that you might die in your
lap pool.
concerned that the remainder of your
teeth
will not last.

concerned about dying but not about
death.

concerned that people will no longer
consider you dangerous when
drunk.

concerned that you will forget who
the enemy is.

concerned that you will forget how to
laugh.

concerned that there will be nothing to
drink in hell.

and concerned you will have to
listen to
one poetry reading
after another
after another . . .

the Los Angeles poets
the New York poets
the Iowa poets

the black poets
the white poets
the Chicano poets
the 3rd world poets

the female poets
the homosexual poets
the lesbian poets
the bisexual poets
the sexless poets
the failed poets
the famous poets
the dead poets
the etc. poets

concerned that the toteboard will
explode into flowers of
shit

and the night will never
come.

Charles the Lion-Hearted

he's 95, lives in a large two story
house.

"they want to send me to a rest
home. 'hell,' I tell them, 'this
IS my home!' "

he speaks of his grandchildren.
he's outlived his
children.

he visits his wife who's also
95.
she's in a rest
home.

"she looks great but she doesn't
know who I am."

he lives on bacon, tomatoes and
breakfast cereal.

he lives on a steep hill.
used to take his little dog for
walks.
the dog died.

he walks alone now,
straight-backed,
carrying an
oak cane.
he's 6 foot two,
lean,
jocular,
imposing.

"they can't wait for me to
die, they want my house
and money.
I'm gonna live just to
spite them."

I see him in his room upstairs
at night
watching tv or
reading.

he was married longer than
most men
live.
he still is
only she doesn't know she's
married.

he sits up in his room
on top of nine and one
half
decades
neither asking nor
giving
mercy.

he is an ocean of
wonder,
he is a shining
rock.

quick of mind,
so quick.

when death comes for
him
it should be
ashamed.

I so want to see that light burning
in that upstairs
window!

when it goes dark
it will be another world
not quite so magic
not quite so good

when it goes dark.

within the dense overcast

the Spaniards had it right and the Greeks had it
right but
my grandmother, heavy with warts, was
confused.

Galileo did more than guess and
Salisbury became what?

the brightness of doom is anybody's
mess as
donkeys and camels are still put to
use.

Cleopatra would have loved
Canadian bacon and
nobody speaks of the
hills of Rome
anymore.

the curve ball curves
and vanilla icecream is always
overstocked.

600,000 people died in the
siege of Leningrad
and we got Shostakovich's
Seventh.

tonight there were gunshots
outside
and I sat and rubbed my
fingers across my greasy
forehead.

palaces, palaces,
and oceans with black

filthy
claws.

the shortest distance between
2 points is
often
intolerable.

who stuck the apple into the
pig's
mouth?
who plucked out his eyes
and baked him
like that?
Cassiodorus?
Cato?

the aviators of May
the buried dogs bones
the marshmallow kisses
the yellowed fleece of sound
the
tack
in the foot.

Virginia is slim.
Madeline is back.
Tina's on the gin.
Becky's on the phone.
don't
answer.

I see you in the closet.
I see you in the dark.
I see you dead.
I see you in the back of a
pick up truck on the
Santa Monica
freeway.

the perfect place to be
in the rain
is in the rain
walking toward a
farmhouse
at one thirty
a.m.
there is a lone light
in an upper
window.
it goes out.
a dog howls.

the nature of the dream is
best interpreted by the
dreamer.

the snail crawls home.
the toes under a blanket
is one of the most magical
sights
ever.

wood is frozen
fire.

my hand is my hand.
my hand is your hand.

the blue shot of
nerve.

Turgenev
Turgenev

the cloud walks toward
me

the pigeon speaks my
name.

corsage

I suppose Jr. High was the worst.
my friend Teddy began going to
various dances
and talking about it all.
his father loaned him the car
for these
functions.

he also had a new wrist watch.
it was still the depression
era and few of us boys
had wrist
watches.

Teddy kept lifting up his wrist
and looking at his
watch.
he did it 3 or 4 times
within a ten minute
period.

"why the hell do you keep
looking at the time?
you going
somewhere?"

"maybe, maybe . . ."

"well, go on then . . ."

"she kissed me at the
doorway, I can still feel her
lips!"

"whose lips?"

"Annabell's, she kissed me
at her door after the
dance!"

"listen, Teddy, let's go down to the
lot and get up a
baseball game."

"I can't get her out of my mind.
her lips were soft,
warm . . ."

"Christ, man, who
cares?"

"I bought her a corsage for
the dance, she looked so
beautiful . . ."

"didn't you slip her any
turkey neck?"

"what?
listen, I'm in love!"

"well, that's what you do
then before somebody
else slams her."

"don't talk that way, I'm
warning you!"

"I can take you, Teddy,
with one ball tied behind
my back."

he looked at his watch:
"I gotta go now . . ."

"gonna go play with yourself
Teddy?"

"look who's talking!
you don't even have a
girl!"

"you don't know what I
have."

"you've got nothing but
your hand."

"I've got two hands, Teddy."

I grabbed him by the shirt and
pulled him in
close.

"and just for laughs I just might
kick your ass, real
good."

"you're just pissed because
you've got
nobody!"

I let him go.

"get out of here . . ."

Teddy turned and
walked off.

he'd gotten off easy that
time.
next time I'd kick his ass
from stem to
stern.

it was 1935.
I was standing in my parents'
back yard.
it was a Saturday
afternoon.
my father was in the house
listening to the radio,
the Trojans were playing
Notre Dame.
my mother was in there
doing something and
nothing.

I walked in through the back
door.
my mother was in the
kitchen.

"Henry, I saw Teddy
leaving.
he's a nice
boy."

"yeah . . ."

"I saw Teddy
all dressed up to go to
the dance.
he looked so
nice!"

"yeah . . ."

"Henry, when are you going
to get a nice girl to take to
a dance?"

"I only dance with them in
bed!"

"YOU DON'T TALK THAT WAY
TO YOUR MOTHER!"

it was my father.
he had been standing there.
it must have been half
time.

"don't bother me," I
said.

"I'LL BOTHER YOU, I'LL BOTHER
YOU SO YOU'LL NEVER TALK THAT
WAY AGAIN!"

"is that right, old man?
come on then, bother
me!"

he stood there.
I stood there.

nothing happened.

"ALL RIGHT," he screamed,
"GO TO YOUR ROOM!
NOW!"

I walked past him, on through
the house and out the
door.

I walked down the street.
I had no money, I had nowhere to
go.
I just kept
walking.

it was a hot summer day
and I just kept walking,

3 blocks, 4 blocks, 5
blocks . . .

then I passed a mongrel dog
going the other
way.

his fur was matted and dirty
and his tongue hung out of
one side of his
mouth.

I stopped, turned and watched
him trot
off.
then I faced the other way and
continued my
journey.

classical music and me

I have no idea how it began.
as a boy I believed that classical music was
for sissies and as a teenager I felt this even
more strongly.

yes, I think it began in this record
store.
I was in my booth listening to whatever I
listened to
at that time.
then I heard some music in the next
booth.
the sounds seemed very strange and
unusual.
I saw the man leave his booth and
return the record to the clerk.
I went to the clerk and asked for that
record.
she handed it to me.
I looked at the cover.

"but," I said, "this is symphony
music."

"yes," said the clerk.

I took the record to my booth
and played it.

never had I heard such
music.
unfortunately, I no longer
remember what that
piece of marvelous
music was.

I purchased the record.
I had a record player in my
room.
I listened to the record
over and over
again.

I was hooked.

soon I found a 2nd hand
record store.
there I found that you could
turn in 3 record albums and
get two back.

I was fairly poor
but most of my money went
for wine and
classical music.
I loved to mix the two
together.

I went through that entire
2nd hand record
store.

my tastes were strange.
I liked Beethoven but
preferred Brahms and
Tchaikovsky.
Borodin didn't work.
Chopin was only good
at moments.
Mozart was only good
when I was feeling
good and I seldom
felt that
way.
Smetana I found
obvious and Sibelius

awesome.
Ives was too self-comfortable.
Goldmark, I felt, was very
underrated.
Wagner was a roaring miracle
of dark energy.
Haydn was love turned loose
into sound.
Handel created things that
took your head and lifted it
to the ceiling.
Eric Coates was unbelievably
cute and astute.
and if you listened to Bach
long enough
you didn't want to listen to
anybody else.
there were dozens
more. . . .

I was on the move from
city to city
and carrying a record player
and records along was
impossible
so I began listening to the
radio
and picking up what I
could.

the problem with the radio
was
that there were a few standard
works they played over and
over.
I heard them too often
and could anticipate each note
before it
arrived.
but the good part was

that, at times, I heard new
music that I had never heard
before by composers I had
never heard of, read about.
I was surprised at the many
composers, fairly unknown,
at least to me, who could
produce these wondrous
and stirring
works.
works that I would never
hear again.

I have continued to listen to
classical music via the radio
for decades.
I am listening as I write
this to Mahler's 9th.
Mahler was always one
of my favorites.
it's possible to listen to
his works again and
again without
tiring of
them.

through the women, through
the jobs, through the horrible
times and the good times,
through deaths, through every-
thing, in and out of hospitals,
in and out of love, through the
decades that have gone so
swiftly
there have been so many
nights of listening
to classical music on the
radio.
almost every
night.

I wish I could remember the name of
the piece I first heard in that
record booth
but it evades me.
for some odd reason I do
remember the conductor:
Eugene Ormandy.
one of the
finest.

now Mahler is in the room
with me
and the chills run up my
arms, reach the back
of my neck . . .
it's all so unbelievably
splendid,
splendid!
and I can't read a note of
music.
But I have found a part of
the world
like no other part of the
world.

it gave heart to my
life, helped me get
to
here.

transport

I was a scraggly bum most of my
life
and to get from one city to another
I took the buses.
I don't know how many times I
saw the Grand Canyon,
going east to west
and west to east.
it was just dusty windows,
the backs of necks, stop-offs at
intolerable eating places
and always the old
constipation
blues.
and once, a half-assed romance
with no socially redeeming
value.

then I found myself riding the
trains.
the food was beautiful
and the restrooms were
lovely
and I stayed in the bar
cars.
some of them were
so grand:
round curving picture
windows
and large overhead
domes,
the sun shone right on
down through your
glass
and at night you could
get
stinko

and watch the stars and
the moon ride
right along with
you.
and the best, since there was more
space
people weren't forced
to speak to
you.

then after the trains I found
myself on the
jetliners,
quick trips to cities and
back.
I was like many of the
others:
I had a briefcase
and was writing on pieces
of paper.
I was on the hustle.
and I hustled and hounded the
stewardesses for drink after
drink.
the food and the view were
bad.
and the people tended to
talk to you
but there were ways to
discourage
that.
the worst about flying was that
there were people waiting for
you at the airports.
baggage was no problem:
you had your carry-on bag,
change of underwear, socks,
one shirt, toothbrush, razor,
liquor.

then the jetliners stopped.
you stayed in the city,
you shacked with unsavory
ladies and you purchased a
series of old cars.
you were much luckier with the
cars than with the
ladies.
you bought the cars for a
song
and drove them with a classic
abandon.
they never needed an oil
change and they lasted and
lasted.
on one the springs were
broken.
on another they stuck up
out of the seat and into your
ass.
one had no reverse
gear.
this was good for me,
it was like playing a game of
chess—
keeping your King from getting
checkmated.
another would only start
when parked on a
hill.
there was one where the
lights wouldn't go on until you
hit a bump
HARD.

of course, they all died
finally.
and it was always a true
heartbreaker for me when

I had to watch them towed off
to the junkyard.

another I lost when it was impounded
on a drunk driving
rap.
they sent me an impound bill that was
four times larger than the purchase
price
so I let them keep
it.

the best car I ever had was the one
my first wife gave me when divorcing
me.
it was two years old,
as old as our marriage.

but the last car was (and is)
the very best, purchased new for
$30,000 cash. (well, I wrote
them a check).
it has everything: air bag,
anti-lock brakes, everything.

also, 2 or 3 times a year
people send a limousine
so we can attend various
functions.
these are very nice
because you can drink like
hell and not worry about the
drunk tank.

but I'm going to bypass that
private plane, that private
boat.
upkeep and rental space
can be a real pain in the
butt.

I'll tell you one thing, though,
one night not so long
ago
I had a dream that I
could fly.
I mean, just by working
my arms and my legs
I could fly through the
air
and I did.
there were all these people
on the ground,
they were reaching up their
arms and trying to pull me
down
but
they couldn't do
it.

I felt like pissing on
them.
they were so
jealous.

all they had to do was
to work their way
slowly up to it
as I had
done.

such people think
success grows on
trees.

you and I,
we know
better.

betrayed

the big thrill
was being quite young and
reading *Of Time and the
River*
by Thomas Wolfe.
what a fat and wondrous
book!
I read it again and
again.

then a couple of decades
went by
and I read the book
again.

I disliked the poetic prose
right off.
I put the book down and
looked about the
room.

I felt cheated.

the thrill was gone.

I decided to leave town.

I was in Los Angeles.

two days later I was sitting on a
Greyhound bus
going to Miami.

and I had a pint of whiskey
in one pocket
and a paperback copy of
Fathers and Sons
in the
other.

torched-out

the worst was closing the bars at
2 a.m.
with my lady.
going home to get a couple hours
sleep,
then as a substitute postal carrier
to be on call at
5:30 a.m.
sitting there with the other
subs
along the little ledge
outside the magazine
cases.

too often given a route to
case and carry,
starting 15 or 20 minutes
late,
the sweat pouring down
your face,
gathering under the
armpits.
you're dizzy, sick,
trying to get the case
up, pull it down and
sack it for the truck to
pick up.

you worked on sheer
nerve,
reaching down into the
gut,
flailing, fighting
as the last minutes,
the last
seconds

rushed toward
you.

then to get on the
route with the people
and the dogs,
to make the rounds
on a new
route,
making your legs
go,
making your feet
walk
as the sun baked
you alive,
you fought through
your first
round
with 6 or 7 more to
go.
never time for lunch,
you'd get a write-up
if you were 5 minutes
late.
a few too many write-
ups and you were
finished,
they moved you
out.

it was a living, a
deathly
living, to somehow
finish your route,
come in and often
be told
you were assigned
to the night pick-
up run, another
ball-buster.

or
if you got out of that
to drive on in
to your place
to find your lady
already drunk,
dirty dishes in the
sink,
the dog unfed,
the flowers unwatered,
the bed
unmade,
the ashtrays full of
punched-out
lipstick-smeared
cigarettes.

then to get in the tub
with a beer.
you were no longer
young,
you were no longer
anything,
just worn down and
out
with your lady in the
other room
lisping inanities and
insanities,
pouring her glasses
of cheap
wine.

you were always going
to get rid of her,
you were working on
that,
you were caught between
the post office and
her,

it was the vise of
death,
each side crushing in
upon you.

"Jesus, baby, please,
please, just shut up for
a little while . . . "

"ah, you asshole!
what're you doing in
there, playing with
yourself?"

to come roaring out
of that tub, all the impossibilities
of that day and that life
corkscrewing through you
ripping away
everything.

out of that tub,
a naked, roaring rocket
of battered body and
mind:

"YOU GOD DAMNED WHORE,
WHAT DO YOU KNOW ABOUT
ANYTHING?
SITTING THERE ON YOUR
DEAD ASS AND
SUCKING AT THE VINO!"

to rush into the other room,
looking all about,
the walls whirling,
the entire world tilting in
against you.

"DON'T HIT ME! DON'T HIT
ME!
YOU'D HIT ME BUT YOU
WOULDN'T HIT A
MAN!"

"HELL NO, I WOULDN'T
HIT A MAN, YOU THINK
I'M CRAZY?"

to grab the bottle from
her,
to drain damn near
half of it.
to find another bottle,
open it,
pour a tall waterglass
full,
then to smash the glass
against a
wall,
to explode it like
that
in purple glory.

to find a new glass,
sit down and pour a
full one.

she'd be quiet
then.
we'd drink an
hour or so
like that.

then, to get
dressed,
cigarette dangling,
you are feeling somewhat
better.

then you are moving
toward the
door.

"hey! where the hell
you going?"

"I'm going to the fucking
bar!"

"not without me!
not without me, buster!"

"all right, get your ass
into gear!"

to walk there together.
to get our stools.
to sit before the long mirror.
the mirror you always hated to
look into.

to tell the bartender,
"vodka 7."

to have her tell the bartender,
"scotch and water."

everything was far away
then,
the post office, the world,
the past and the
future.

to have our drinks arrive.
to take the first hit in the
dark bar.

life couldn't get any
better.

the word

there was Auden, I don't remember
which small room I first read him
in
and there was Spender and I don't
know which small room
either
and then there was Ezra
and I remember that room,
there was a torn screen
that the flies came through
and it was Los Angeles
and the woman said to me,
"Jesus Christ, you reading those
Cantos again!"
she liked e. e. cummings, though,
she thought he was really
good and she was
right.

I remember when I read Turgenev,
though, I had just come out of the
drunk tank and I was living
alone
and I thought he was really a
subtle and funny son of a
bitch.

Hemingway I read everywhere,
sometimes a few times over
and he made me feel brave
and tough
until one day
it all just stopped cold for me
and worse than that,
Ernie became an
irritant.

my Jeffers period was sometime
in Los Angeles, some room, some
job,
the same woman was back
and she said,
"Jesus, how can you read this
crap?"
one time when she was gone
I found many magazines
under the bed.
I pulled them out
and found that the contents were
all about murder
and it was all about women
who were tortured, killed,
dismembered and so
forth with the
lurid photos
in black and
white.
that stuff wasn't for
me.

my first encounter with Henry
Miller was via paperback
on a bus through Arizona.
he was great when he stuck
to reality
but when he got ethereal
when he got to philosophizing
he got as dry and boring as
the passing
landscape.
I left him in the men's crapper
at a hamburger
stop.

I got hold of Celine's *Journey*
and read it straight through
while in bed eating crackers.

I kept reading, eating the
crackers and reading, reading,
laughing out loud,
thinking, at last I've met a man
who writes better than
I.
I finished the book and then
drank much water.
the crackers swelled up
inside of me
and I got the worst
god damned stomach
ache of my
life.

I was living with my first
wife.
she worked for the L.A.
Sheriff's Dept.
and she came in to
find me doubled up
and moaning.

"Oh, what happened?"

"I've just read the world's
greatest
writer!"

"But you said *you* were."

"I'm second, baby . . ."

I read F. D.'s *Notes from the
Underground*
in a small El Paso
library
after sleeping the night
on a park bench

during a sand
storm.
after reading that book
I knew I had a long way
to go as a
writer.

I don't know where I read
T. S. Eliot.
he made a small dent
which soon ironed
out.

there were many rooms,
many books,
D. H. Lawrence, Gorky,
A. Huxley, Sherwood
Anderson, Sinclair Lewis,
James Thurber, Dos Passos,
etc
Kafka.
Schopenhauer, Nietzsche,
Rabelais.
Hamsun.

as a very young man
I worked as a shipping clerk,
made the bars at
night,
came into the roominghouse,
went to bed
and read the
books.
I had 3 or 4 of them in
bed with me (what a
man!) and then I would
sleep.

my landlady finally told
me, "You know, you read those

books in bed and about every
hour or so one of them will
fall to the floor.
You are keeping everybody
awake!"

(I was on the 3rd floor.)

what days and nights those
were.

now I can't read anything,
not even the newspaper.
and, of course, I can't watch
tv except for the boxing
matches.
I do hear some news
on the car radio
while driving the freeway
and waiting for the
traffic
reports.

but you know, my former
life as a bibliophile, it
possibly kept me from
murdering somebody,
myself
included.
it kept me from being an
industrialist.
it allowed me to endure
some women
that most men would never
be able to live
with.
it gave me space, a
pause.

it helped me to write
this

(in this room,
like the other rooms)

perhaps for some young man
now
needing
to laugh at the
impossibilities
which are here
always
after we are
not.

shooting the moon in the eye

it was just a small room, no bathroom,
hot plate, bed, 2 chairs, a bed, sink,
phone in hall.
I was on the 2nd floor of a hotel.
I had a job.
I got in about 6:30 p.m.
and by 8 p.m.
there would be 4 or 5 people
in the room,
all drunks,
all drinking wine.
sometimes there would be
6 or 7.
most of them sat on the
bed.
oh, there was a radio,
we played the radio,
drank and
talked.

it was strange, there was
always a sense of
excitement there,
some laughter and
sometimes serious
arguments that were
somewhat
stupid.

we were never asked
to be quiet,
the manager never
bothered us,
or the
police.
with an exception
or two,

there were no
physical
confrontations.
I'd always call an
end to the parties
around 3 a.m.

"ah, come on Hank!
we're just getting
started!"

"come on, come
on, everybody
out!"

and,
with an exception
or two,
I always slept
without a
lady.

we called
that place,
the Hotel from
Hell.

I had no idea
what we were
trying to
do.

I think we were
just celebrating
being
alive.

that small room
full of smoke and
music and

voices,
night after night
after
night.

the poor, the mad,
the lost.

we lit up that hotel
with our twisted
souls
and it loved
us.

nirvana

not much chance,
completely cut loose from
purpose,
he was a young man
riding a bus
through North Carolina
on the way to
somewhere
and it began to snow
and the bus stopped
at a little cafe
in the hills
and the passengers
entered.

he sat at the counter
with the others,
he ordered and the
food arrived.
the meal was
particularly
good
and the
coffee.

the waitress was
unlike the women
he had
known.
she was unaffected,
there was a natural
humor which came
from her.
the fry cook said
crazy things.
the dishwasher,
in back,

laughed, a good
clean
pleasant
laugh.

the young man watched
the snow through the
windows.

he wanted to stay
in that cafe
forever.

the curious feeling
swam through him
that everything
was
beautiful
there,
that it would always
stay beautiful
there.

then the bus driver
told the passengers
that it was time
to board.

the young man
thought, I'll just sit
here, I'll just stay
here.

but then
he rose and followed
the others into the
bus.

he found his seat
and looked at the cafe
through the bus
window.

then the bus moved
off, down a curve,
downward, out of
the hills.

the young man
looked straight
forward.
he heard the other
passengers
speaking
of other things,
or they were
reading
or
attempting to
sleep.

they had not
noticed
the
magic.

the young man
put his head to
one side,
closed his
eyes,
pretended to
sleep.
there was nothing
else to do—
just listen to the
sound of the
engine,
the sound of the
tires
in the
snow.

an invitation

hey Chinaski:

I am a filmmaker in the Hollywood area and I am currently making a movie in which I would like to include you.

The nature of the movie is about an alcoholic Satan who decides to leave hell for a while and have a vacation in Hollywood.

This particular version of Satan is a fun guy who can't get enough booze, SLUTS, or adventure.

Satan, while in Hollywood looks up his old buddies (Ghosts) Richard Burton, Errol Flynn and Idi Amin (still alive). He proceeds to get smashed with these guys and they all pass out on him so he needs to look up a mortal worthy of drinking with him (YOU).

The scene I have envisioned with you would be to be sitting around a crummy joint, drinking Mezcal and playing Russian Roulette with Satan while 2 big fat chicks are slapping each other with Salamis. I would want everybody in the scene to be SMASHED.

I can tell you now that I couldn't pay you anything up front xcept Booze and adventure.

—However—

I am going to hopefully be able to release this movie one day and would be happy to work out a contractual agreement that would arrange a royalty rate—(if you are interested.)

And thanks for mentioning in your writing, KNUT HAMSUN.

he has turned out to be one of my
faves.
And just remember,
WHEN IN DOUBT,
PASS OUT!

batting order:

Hemingway's been in a slump,
can't hit a curve ball
anymore,
I'm dropping him to the 6th
spot.
I'm putting Celine in
cleanup,
he's inconsistent but when
he's good there's no
better.
Hamsun I'm going to use
in the number 3 spot,
he hits them hard and
often.
lead-off, well, lead-off
I'll use e. e. cummings,
he's fast, can beat out a
bunt.
I'll use Pound in the
number two spot, Ezra
is one of the better
hit and run men
in the business.
the 5 spot I'll give to
Dostoevsky,
he's a heavy hitter, great with
men on base.
the 7 spot I'll give to Robinson
Jeffers, can you think of anybody
better?
he can drill a rock
350 feet.
the 8 spot, I've got my
catcher, J. D. Salinger,
if we can find
him.
and pitching?

how about Nietzsche?
he's strong!
been breaking all the tables
in the training
room.

coaches?

I'll take Kierkegaard and
Sartre,
gloomy fellows,
but none know this
game better.

when we field this team,
it's all over,
gentlemen.

we're going to kick some
ass, most likely
yours.

the open canvas

listening to organ music on the radio
tonight,
the door to the small balcony is
open,
it is 11:07 p.m., cold, a night of
silence except for the
radio, the
organ music,
and I get this vision
of a thin, tall man at the key-
board, he is more than pale, al-
most a chalky
white.
the music boils in the
gloom.
the walls about him are
unpainted, cold,
austerely
indifferent.

a full glass of wine sits
untouched
on a rough hand-made table
to his
right.

the music seeps through his
bones,
centuries bend and
unwind as the invisible dog
of darkness
walks by
in a half circle
behind him,
then blends into
neurons.

the man continues to
play.
the world turns upsidedown
with a fixed gentleness
but the walls, the man,
the sounds continue
as before.

then the world returns to its
natural course.

one tonality breeds
another.
the sounds of black strings
of beads.
the sound is one
yet not one.

then the music
stops.

the man sits.

he is thoughtless.

the keys of the organ assume
an immensity.

the walls about him move away
faster than the eye
can note,
then they
return.

the man coughs, looks to
his left,
looks down,
touches the keys and
is taken
again.

in the shadow of the rose

branching out, grubbing down,
taking stairways down to hell,
reestablishing the vanishing
point, trying a different
bat, a different stance, alter-
ing diet and manner of
walking, readjusting the
system, photographing your
dinosaur dream,
driving your machine with
more grace and care,
noticing the flowers talking
to you,
realizing the gigantic agony
of the terrapin,
you pray for rain like an
Indian,
slide a fresh clip into the
automatic,
turn out the lights and
wait.

Photo: Michael Montfort

CHARLES BUKOWSKI is one of America's best-known contemporary writers of poetry and prose, and, many would claim, its most influential and imitated poet. He was born in Andernach, Germany, to an American soldier father and a German mother in 1920, and brought to the United States at the age of three. He was raised in Los Angeles and lived there for fifty years. He published his first story in 1944 when he was twenty-four and began writing poetry at the age of thirty-five. He died in San Pedro, California, on March 9, 1994, at the age of seventy-three, shortly after completing his last novel, *Pulp* (1994).

During his lifetime he published more than forty-five books of poetry and prose, including the novels *Post Office* (1971), *Factotum* (1975), *Women* (1978), *Ham on Rye* (1982), and *Hollywood* (1989). Among his most recent books are the posthumous editions of *What Matters Most Is How Well You Walk Through the Fire* (1999), *Open All Night: New Poems* (2000), *Beerspit Night and Cursing: The Correspondence of Charles Bukowski and Sheri Martinelli, 1960–1967* (2001), and *The Night Torn Mad with Footsteps: New Poems* (2001).

All of his books have now been published in translation in over a dozen languages and his worldwide popularity remains undiminished. In the years to come, Ecco will publish additional volumes of previously uncollected poetry and letters.